BR CLOUGH

THE LOST TAPES

BRIAN CLOUGH
THE LOST TAPES

MARCUS ALTON

DB
PUBLISHING

Dedicated to my wonderful wife, Sarah, for her support
and good humour.

A special mention to my parents, Margaret and David, who encouraged my
writing career from an early age. Dad's memory lives on in the following pages,
as well as in some great recordings I found while researching this book.

Part of the proceeds of this book will go to two charities: the NSPCC and
Nottinghamshire Hospice.

Front and back cover images kindly supplied by Rogues Gallery.
It's well worth a visit: www.rogues.gallery

First published 2023 by DB Publishing, an imprint of JMD Media Ltd,

Nottingham, United Kingdom.

ISBN 9781780916309

Printed in the UK

Contents

About the Author

'The world's leading authority on Brian Clough' – the International Soccer Network

Brian Clough once told Marcus during a live radio interview that he liked to see his smiling face because it brightened up an otherwise dull and wet winter's morning. The former BBC and commercial radio journalist interviewed Cloughie several times and has previously written four books about him. He is the founder and editor of the non-profit tribute website, brianclough.com, which he set-up in August 2000, and hosts the Cloughie podcast, *Green Jumper*.

As an award winning journalist and public relations expert, Marcus's journalistic and writing career has spanned more than 35 years with the BBC (TV, radio and online), commercial radio, print journalism and PR. During his time with the BBC he presented several radio programmes, including his own chat show, interviewing celebrities, politicians and sports stars.

Brian Clough: The Lost Tapes is Marcus's fifth book about Brian Clough. Speaking engagements have included several book festivals, with his 'In The Top One' event attracting a sell-out audience at Newark Book Festival. He has also appeared at 'An Evening With …' at Waterstones and held signing sessions at WHSmith. Marcus wrote a regular column for the Nottingham Forest matchday magazine, entitled 'View from the Brian Clough Stand'.

The books by Marcus – including Amazon best-sellers – have helped to raise money for various charities, including the NSPCC, the Royal British Legion, Diabetes UK and a hospital charity. Marcus presented a cheque for £7,500 to the children's cancer ward at the Queen's Medical Centre in Nottingham, on behalf of the Brian Clough Memorial Fund.

Following the passing of Brian Clough in 2004, Marcus was the driving force behind the campaign for a bronze statue of Cloughie in Nottingham city centre, forming a committee of volunteers who smashed their fundraising target in just 18 months. The statue was unveiled by Barbara Clough in November 2008 and has become a landmark in the city, attracting visitors from around the world.

In February 2021, Marcus launched the Clough tribute podcast *Green Jumper*, which has since been downloaded thousands of times by listeners around the world. Guests have included many former players, journalists and authors. The podcast is available on all major podcast platforms, including Apple, Google, Amazon and Spotify.

brianclough.com
@1BrianClough on X/Twitter and facebook.com/cloughie1935
Instagram: @cloughie1935
youngman@brianclough.com

A Note From the Author

While writing this book and searching through my archives, I came across some wonderful Clough quotes which I've included for posterity. Some are in print for the first time, having initially been recorded in radio or television interviews and personal appearances.

Here are just a few of them:

On player discipline, 'I used to look up at Larry Lloyd and think that one of these days he's going to belt me and I'll finish up in the Trent. But I would have had no trouble in the Trent because I had a path I used to walk across.'

On meeting the Queen, 'I think she was looking forward to meeting me.'

On signing talented players without spending a fortune, 'I signed Roger Davies for two lorry loads of plums. He came from Worcester – good plum-growing territory.'

On politicians, 'We pay their wages and they make such a mess of it and then they come back and ask us to do it all again. You've either got to be as thick as hell to do that – or a very talented man.'

On job insecurity, 'The only job I can think of that is less secure than football manager is snow-clearing.'

On where his loyalties would lie, before watching a derby match between the Rams and the Reds, 'The only problem I've got is deciding which board of directors to sit with – because they're all bums!'

On winning his first honours in management, at Derby County, 'It's like your first girlfriend. You never forget her, do you?'

On Sir Alex Ferguson, 'He took me into his office and gave me a drop of sherry. I told him I didn't think they were still making thimbles.'

On his managerial philosophy, 'Put it in a book and it'll replace the Bible in every hotel room in the country.'

PS: Over the years I've been extremely flattered that many of the quotes I collated on the tribute website have been reproduced by newspapers and magazines. If you're a journalist or writer and wish to include some of the quotes collated in this book, please give it a mention and thereby help the good causes which will benefit from the book's sales. Thanks very much. M.A.

Twenty Years

It's hard to believe that 2024 will mark 20 years since the football world was in mourning for the Miracle Manager. Fans around the world will remember where they were when they heard the sad news that Brian Clough had passed away on 20 September, 2004. I was on holiday in Paris when I received a phone call from a BBC colleague to tell me.

During the following 48 hours my mobile phone was receiving call after call with requests for interviews. Bearing in mind these were days before hotel wifi, the reception staff recommended an internet cafe about 20 minutes away, where I could pay an hourly rate to update the tribute website.

In the years since Cloughie died, there have been so many tributes paid to his footballing genius and his generosity off the pitch. Although the campaign I organised for him to receive a knighthood didn't receive support in time at government level, I will always be grateful that Brian knew about it before he passed away. It's still a massive injustice that the government didn't act sooner to bestow the widely supported honour while he was alive.

It seems it's only in retrospect that many people realise the scale of what Cloughie achieved – such a lot of awards and recognition actually came much later. And that's a fact Brian recognised during his retirement, when he was asked to attend award ceremonies and special dinners. I listened back to a recording of him on a radio programme in 2001 when he said, 'I sometimes think you get awards too late. People don't recognise how good you were.'

During this recording he recalled how he had presented an award to Sir Tom Finney, long after the former England and Preston forward had retired. Clough admired Sir Tom, who had taken the young Middlesbrough player under his wing when they were both in the England squad in 1959. During a trip to Russia, a nervous Clough spilt his breakfast down his trousers and was reassured by Sir Tom, who arranged for the pair of 'flannels' to be cleaned. It was an act of generosity that Brian never forgot. 'He looked after me,' said Cloughie, who then referred to what happened when he had presented an award to Sir Tom many years later.

'He turned round and said, "Brian, I'm getting more awards now than I ever got when I was a player. I never got anything when I was in my 20s and 30s." And it happens like that. They don't realise how good you were.'

Brian went on to describe how he had been dropped from the team when he didn't score in five matches. Yet he managed to get 43 goals in that same season. 'I know what Tom Finney was talking about then, because I'm getting bits and bobs of awards now, a long, long time afterwards.'

Four years after he passed away, I was invited to report on Cloughie's induction into the Hall of Fame at a National Football Museum evening in Liverpool. Brian's son Nigel was presented with the award by Nottingham Forest's European Cup-winning captain John McGovern.

At a news conference before the event, I interviewed Nigel who described the award as a huge honour. He said his dad would have been extremely proud, 'He would have loved to have been here in such company, with so many people who he had an immense amount of respect for in his business. I think pretty much everyone who's anyone in European football in the last 30 years is here. A lot of people he competed against and a lot of them he supported over the years.'

Among the other managers inducted was the late Liverpool boss Bob Paisley. Nigel said his father often spoke with affection and admiration about Paisley. Former Liverpool defender Phil Neal was among the guests and told me that he was pleased that both Clough and Paisley were being honoured (they were the only two managers out of five being inducted who had not received knighthoods – the others were Sir Alex Ferguson, Sir Bobby Robson and Sir Matt Busby). On Clough's inclusion, Neal said, 'It is justified in recognising Brian Clough for what he did for the national game let alone Nottingham Forest too.'

There are now three statues of Cloughie – in Middlesbrough, Nottingham and Derby. It was, quite literally, a monumental task to raise the money for the one in Nottingham, but the small group of fundraisers I gathered together smashed the target in 18 months, long before the days of online donation pages. It's still a source of huge pride to see visitors from around the world taking selfies next to the bronze sculpture. At the unveiling ceremony, Barbara Clough said Brian would have been amazed at the very thought of a statue. And in a TV documentary Nigel summed up the overall sentiment perfectly when he said, 'In many years to come, there will be people in Nottingham who'll be walking around, and tourists from different countries, and they will ask who is that fella, and someone might just explain who it is and why it's there.' Mrs Clough told the programme, 'I think he would be so pleased. I think he would be in tears, probably, if he saw that. I'm sure he will see it.'

It might be some two decades since the football genius left us, but the recognition and the admiration are greater than ever. Trevor Francis, who tragically passed away as I was completing this book, put it beautifully when, in 2009, he said, 'He intrigues me. That intrigue and mystique has remained. That is why, since he finished management, in the eyes of the public he has become even more important.'

Paul Hart and family with Brian Clough after the defender signed at the City Ground. (credit: Nottingham Post)

Brian Clough's tribute to Paul Hart

(Quotes from August and November 2001):

'Paul is someone I always liked, as a player and as a person, and I firmly believe he possesses the right football instincts.

'He's got all the credentials. He's got the pedigree and he's well-liked. He knows the game – he's been in it long enough now. I noticed since I last saw him on television that he's lost a few more strands of his hair, but that applies to us all. He's got everything going for him.'

Foreword by Paul Hart

When I was told that Brian Clough wanted to sign me, I was absolutely delighted. I was at Leeds United and I met him in the manager's office there. I knocked on the door and said, 'Good evening, Mr Clough.' But he said, 'Don't call me Mr Clough, call me Brian.' But I thought it was a trap! I never did call him Brian throughout our time together.

Reading his comments about me, reproduced in this book, brings back some great memories. I really enjoyed my time working with the Gaffer. He was a very clever man and he had core values which he imposed on his players. When I started coaching young players at Leeds United's academy, I took those Nottingham Forest values and used them. Things like not feigning injury, not swearing at referees and not pulling shirts. And the importance of saying 'yes please' and 'no thank you'.

When I came back to Nottingham Forest as academy manager and then manager, he used to come to the games and sit with me in the office and we'd talk. He would ask me about what I was doing and how I was doing it. He never judged, but he was there. To have somebody like him, knowing that he was in your corner if you needed something, made me feel I was a very lucky man.

It's good to know that the Gaffer's memory is kept alive through the tributes and recollections Marcus has compiled. His *Green Jumper* podcast was also a pleasure to be part of and is well worth a listen. I hope you enjoy reading this collection of memories from the archives.

The Warm-Up

Carefully slipping the cassette into the small, portable tape machine brought back memories of distant days. I was instantly taken back several decades – not only from listening to the archive audio recorded on the tape, but by the simple act of placing the cassette in the machine and pressing the 'Play' button.

I was a very lucky lad when, just eight years old, I was given a tape recorder for Christmas. Santa had been extremely well briefed that year. After winning a competition on the new independent radio station, Radio Trent, and being invited into the studio to be presented with the prize (a boxed set of three Wombles albums!), I had become fascinated with all things involving radio shows. That included listening to and recording them – as well as later 'presenting' my own programme using two turntables and a little mixing desk in my bedroom.

The little tape recorder I received on Christmas morning in 1975 opened the door to a wonderful world I would later do my best to earn a living from. My first task using that magical machine was to record songs off the radio, perfecting the knack of pressing 'Record' and 'Play' simultaneously at just the right time.

A few years later, having mastered the art of avoiding the presenter's voice at the beginning and end of my recordings from the radio, I went a step further. Mesmerised by the charisma of Brian Clough, and with the idea of being a radio presenter firmly in my head, I would pretend I was interviewing him.

Still just a young lad, I would record his interviews off the radio or television and on to my little mono cassette recorder. Carefully timing the questions and his answers, I would record over the interviewer's comments to make it sound as if I was interviewing Cloughie himself. I have to laugh to myself these days, following decades of professional broadcasting, and fully admit that the 'editorial guidelines' on Midland Radio (my fictitious radio station, but an idea ahead of its time!) were extremely vague. The station would do whatever I decided. A bit like Cloughie running a football club, I suppose!

Decades later, here I was listening to one of the *genuine* face-to-face interviews I'd recorded with Brian Clough. Luckily, despite having recorded it in the days of reel-to-reel recorders, I had made a copy of it on cassette – and here it was, having been buried underneath a pile of cardboard boxes in the loft at home. It was in an old shoebox, along with a collection of many other old cassettes and various other recordings which had not seen daylight for many years. In some of the boxes were cuttings of newspaper reports and magazine articles featuring Cloughie.

This collection of old recordings includes his first studio-based football phone-in and an appearance at a fans' forum in which he was typically outspoken, as well as a video of one of my meetings with Old Big 'Ead.

I hadn't played these tapes for years but the Covid lockdown gave me the impetus to have a sort-out and look for some of the memorabilia I'd collected over the years. This book is the result. I hope that, like me, the journey back in time – accompanied by some of the people involved – puts a smile on your face too.

1

Radio Gold

The voice was unmistakable. The visit was unprecedented. I could see him sitting in front of a microphone in one of the radio studios at the BBC in Nottingham. It was the first time he had taken part in a studio-based, hour-long football phone-in. The live broadcast was about to start in about ten minutes and – standing in the neighbouring production area – I listened to some of the off-air comments as we edged closer to the moment that the red 'on-air' light would flash into life.

I was working in the BBC Radio Nottingham newsroom on this particular day in May 2000. Nervous excitement had been building-up among some colleagues for most of the day, knowing that the iconic former football manager Brian Clough was due to make this momentous visit. What would he say? Would he be in good form? Was it wise to broadcast the show 'live' considering his reputation for being unpredictable and outspoken? We would soon find out.

As the clock ticked down to the start of the programme, I seized the opportunity to have a quick word with the special guest. Opening the heavy studio door, I checked that the presenter, my colleague Mark Shardlow, was fine and had everything he needed for the programme. I then introduced myself to the man sitting alongside him.

'Hello Mr Clough, it's good to see you looking well. Thanks for coming in to see us. Could I have a quick photo before the show starts, please?' I kept it short and sweet and hoped for the best.

'Of course you can, son,' came the reply with a big smile. 'And call me Brian.'

Sitting next to Mr Clough (I still didn't call him Brian!) was his former European Cup-winning striker Garry Birtles. With the help of a colleague, I got a great photo with them which I still cherish. Then, making myself scarce so that Mark could prepare for the show's opening, I quietly slipped back into the technical room to help with the production of this historic broadcast.

More than 20 years after the original programme was broadcast, I was looking through a box of Cloughie memorabilia when I came across an old recording of parts of the phone-in. It was included on a cassette tape of various recordings I'd compiled all those years ago. Listening back was a real treat. The incisive and often witty comments were still as relevant today as they had been then. It seemed as if the Miracle Manager had never left us.

Reflecting on the show decades later, Mark told me that Cloughie's appearance had been weeks in the planning. The regular Monday evening phone-in was still in its infancy at the time. The usual guest was Forest legend Garry, who loved chatting to the listeners, long before he became a familiar pundit on Sky Sports.

Behind the scenes, Garry was asked whether he could persuade Brian to appear on the weekly phone-in. The former Nottingham Forest and Manchester United forward struck gold.

Mark told me, 'It's hard to believe it now, but at that time there were very few football phone-ins. After about a year, we thought we'd see if Garry could get Brian to come along and be a guest.'

There's no doubt that Cloughie was absolutely *made* for the football phone-in format. 'He would have been the king of phone-ins if they'd been around 20 or 30 years earlier,' added Mark.

Nevertheless, his unpredictability meant that even an experienced radio and television presenter had to prepare thoroughly for this live broadcast.

'You really didn't know what you were going to get,' Mark told me. 'As a presenter, you knew you had to be on your mettle and you needed to plan for lots of scenarios. There's a lot to think about before the show begins: what do I do if "A" happens, what do I say if "B" happens?

'Of course, when the programme went live, we didn't need any plan "C", "D", "E", "F" or "G". It was all "Plan A" and it was all Brian Clough.'

Mark laughed as he recalled the first caller. 'It went something like, "Hello Brian, it's an honour to speak to you." And the response was "Son, thanks, get on with it."'

That first caller was introduced as Alan from Bulwell. His question, 'Which player was the most influential signing you ever made at Forest?'

Cloughie admitted it was a difficult question. 'I signed good players all the time,' was his initial assessment. 'Any player who came in had to be a good player. There was no point in lowering the standards.'

Then he changed the focus of the question and produced a quote which has since become a classic, 'I signed the ugliest player I ever signed when I signed Kenny Burns. He'd got no teeth.' At that point there was a little chuckle from

Alan in Bulwell, before Brian continued, 'I used to play centre-forward and to have beaten somebody with the ball and then seen Kenny Burns looking at me, I'd have *given* him the ball. He wouldn't have had to take it away from me.' There was more laughter, both from the caller and in the studio.

As a player, Cloughie knew how to sidestep a difficult opponent. As an interviewee, he was an expert in sidestepping a difficult question. 'He was a master of dodging a question with a witty reply,' said Mark.

One of the best examples came during the conversation with a caller introduced as Dave in Brinsley, who began by telling Cloughie, 'Forget all the Shanklys and the Fergusons and all of them, you're the greatest. To us Forest fans, you are God.'

High praise indeed. With the unadulterated adulation out of the way, Dave asked his question, which was carefully sidestepped. He wanted to know who Brian's favourite Forest player had been.

'I didn't have one,' said Clough.

'You didn't?' questioned Dave.

'No. They were all the same to me. I didn't like any of them.'

There was spontaneous laughter in the studio and from Dave. Then Clough expanded on his answer to clarify what he really meant, 'They were all the same. I liked their skills and I liked their particular forte.' Names such as Birtles, Robertson, Lloyd and Burns were then mentioned as examples, before the punchline was delivered with aplomb, 'Hey, did we have a bad one?'

It was another perfect diversion from the original question. A clever way of avoiding any admission of having a 'favourite' member of the team.

'He was super sharp,' recalled Mark. 'He was playing to the crowd. It was like a one-two-three put-down. He was brilliant at that.'

The 'crowd', or the listeners, must have been lapping it up. Perhaps that explained why, initially, it seemed that they preferred to listen rather than actually pick up the phone and call. The rate at which people were calling was very slow at first.

Another explanation could be that listeners were actually awestruck and couldn't bring themselves to speak to someone they regarded – in the words of Dave in Brinsley – as 'a God'.

I remember how, years later, grown men who had queued at a Cloughie book signing were almost lost for words when they met their hero. One fan described how his hand was still shaking as he attempted to sign the credit card slip (there was no contactless payment in those days!).

Mark told me, 'It's fair to say that many people who phoned in were besides themselves. They were trembling at the prospect of speaking to such an icon.

They couldn't believe they were talking to this man who had done such wonderful things for Forest, the city and the county.'

As the phone-in continued, I'd made my way back into the Newsroom, on the same floor as the studio in which a football legend was holding court. I turned up the volume on a small speaker which sat on one of the tables.

I was listening intently because it was my job to pick out some of the best bits of the programme and put them together in an audio montage for the following morning's BBC Radio Nottingham *Breakfast Show*.

But, behind the scenes, it was becoming clear that the initial burst of callers was starting to dry up. Clough was so entertaining that *listeners* preferred to, well, *listen*.

I realised we needed a way to encourage more people to phone in. It was an hour-long programme and although Mark was adept at asking interesting questions, the whole idea was for Cloughie to speak directly with the fans.

There was only one thing for it. I phoned my dad who I knew would be listening and would jump at the chance of speaking to our special guest. Here was someone who, many years earlier, had waited patiently in the Nottingham Forest car park to secure Brian Clough's autograph and was invited into his office. Cloughie added, 'To Marcus, "Be Good", Brian Clough' to a collection of signatures inside a Forest book which became a treasured Christmas present.

Within a few minutes of my call to Dad, David from Sutton in Ashfield (as he was also known!) had phoned in and helped to get the ball well and truly rolling.

The conversation went something like this:

BC, 'David, good evening to you.'

DA, 'Hello Brian. I saw you the other evening at Mark Crossley's testimonial. You were looking well.'

BC, 'Ah, thank you. I'd got some make-up on.'

DA, 'Was that for the cameras?'

BC, 'Actually I put it on for you and I didn't see you.'

DA, 'Oh well, I saw you – I did wave, but I don't think you saw me.'

BC, 'Well son, when you wave to me it's very difficult. If you put your hand up one way, that's waving. If you turn your hand round and there's two fingers, I tend to ignore it.'

DA, 'No, there's no way I'd put two fingers up to you, Brian.'

BC, 'Ah, there isn't, right. Get on with your question.'

DA, 'I was wondering what advice you'd give David Platt [the new Forest manager]? Do you think that next season he should consolidate or go directly for promotion – and how could he strengthen the side?'

For Cloughie, the answer was simple. Platt had to go for promotion. 'You start the season wanting to better yourself,' he said. It then became clear that the expert storyteller was just warming up as he expanded on the theme of making new signings. Like a theatre performer or comedian gearing up for the punchline, his carefully constructed answer led to one of his classic one-liners.

BC, 'It all depends on who you sign. Now, academically I'm thick, right?'

DA, 'Well, I don't believe that, but if you say so …'

BC, 'Well, that's all right son. If you don't believe it, I'm delighted. I've got no O-Levels and no A-Levels. I've got a couple of MAs, but apart from that … I'm thick.'

At this point we all wondered where the answer was going. Then all became clear as he talked about the foreign players that Platt had signed.

BC, 'If he could just sign somebody in England we knew about. I think the first three he signed were Italians.'

As Brian described how difficult it would be for him to get a basic message across to an Italian player, due to the language barrier, he went on to say, 'Now, I can't even spell spaghetti, never mind talk Italian. Now, how could I tell an Italian how to get the ball?'

In the interests of younger readers, I won't complete the final bit of the answer. It's safe to say it involved a part of his anatomy.

* * *

The amusing exchange between Cloughie and my dad soon prompted more people to phone in. Derek in Warsop was brave enough to ask how Brian had felt when he was sacked by Leeds United after just 44 days in charge.

'Well, I was obviously upset when they sacked me,' came the reply. 'But I became financially secure for the first time in my life. I was born without a penny. Three-pence was my pocket money for a month. When I got the sack, I went home with a cheque because I'd just signed a four-year contract and they paid me up for the four years.'

Then there was some typical Cloughie humour, 'I didn't learn from that experience. If I'd have learned from it, I'd have been a bad manager and got paid every time I got the sack.'

Talking of the sack, Brian was asked what he thought about another management casualty which had just been announced. 'He's been given the chop today – what do you think to that?' enquired Mark.

This gave Brian the ideal hook for his answer, 'Well, I don't like to see any manager get the chop, as you use that word. The only chops I have are Barnsley chops.'

Interviewed the following year, Clough criticised football chairmen who kept sacking their managers. He described a spate of managerial casualties as 'a barmy situation' and said the chairmen were 'a pack of wolves devouring everything in sight'.

He continued, 'The chairmen are not making any improvements because all they're doing is sacking the present managers and re-engaging those who've already had the sack from another club.'

Then came his conclusion, 'There should be a rule that if the manager goes within a year, then the chairman goes with him.'

The phone-in also gave Clough the opportunity to talk about one of the most controversial matches during his 18 years as Nottingham Forest manager. The game is not even mentioned in either of his two autobiographies, but he was ready to talk about it when Nicola from Chester called.

The question was straightforward: what did he think about Forest's controversial defeat to Anderlecht in the UEFA Cup semi-final in 1984? And had he suspected anything untoward at the time? In his reply, Clough got straight to the point. He said his side had been cheated from start to finish.

The Reds had convincingly won the first leg 2-0 at home. But in the return match they had a dubious penalty awarded against them and had a last-gasp goal disallowed, losing 3-2 on aggregate. That late Paul Hart header, controversially ruled out as a goal at the time, would have been enough to win the tie.

Many years later Anderlecht were banned from European competition for a year after admitting they paid the referee. But it came too late for Forest's players who still felt that justice wasn't done.

'We should have gone through to the final and I think we'd have played Tottenham,' Clough told the phone-in. 'But it was a crooked match and he was a crooked referee.'

In an article in *The Guardian* in 2013, journalist Danny Taylor described it as 'one of the great match-fixing scandals of its time' and added that it 'still remains in the small print of the sport's history books'.

Paul Hart told Taylor that he could still remember Clough's demeanour in the dressing room after that second leg in Anderlecht. The usually outspoken manager was 'unusually quiet'. Having always insisted his players shouldn't complain to referees about decisions, it was no surprise that they didn't make more of the controversial outcome at the time.

Said Hart, 'One of the things about Brian Clough's teams was that we were always taught never to complain to referees. So we just got on the plane afterwards and flew home. We had a game that weekend against Stoke City and we just got on with it.'

John Wragg had been covering the match for the *Daily Express* and told Taylor that it had been obvious Clough had suspected something was not right. Said Wragg, 'This was back in the days when everyone mixed and after the game all the players and officials were together in one big room. Cloughie came up to the various journalists, kissed each of us on the cheek and said, "Eh, you know we were cheated, don't you?"'

Those memories were still all too vivid when Cloughie took that call from Nicola. Garry Birtles, sitting beside Brian in the studio, was part of the squad that faced Anderlecht. He was also sitting alongside Brian on the bench that fateful night. He admitted that even recalling the events of that trip to Belgium left a bad taste.

* * *

Thankfully, behind the scenes, the phone lines were now lighting up and Cloughie was in his element, proceeding to regale stories from the glory days. But there was one story which he seemed reluctant to tell – maybe because Garry was sitting next to him.

Karen from Bestwood Park asked what had happened when Clough told Garry to get off the team bus on the way to the airport. It's a story Brian had told many times before. He had previously described how he'd become fed up with Garry complaining about making the trip to the Middle East, including the fact it meant an early start on a Sunday morning. Apparently, Clough was so annoyed he told Garry to get off the coach, flagging down a passing motorist to take him back to the City Ground.

However, despite being asked several times in the phone-in to recall what happened that morning, Brian wasn't going to recount all the details on this occasion.

Initially, Karen got straight to the point and asked Garry what he thought 'when Brian kicked you off the coach' on the way to the airport. Without hesitation, Mark took it a step further and directed the question at Cloughie, 'Brian, why did you kick him off the bus?'

'Well, literally speaking, I didn't kick him,' said Brian. 'I just said, "Get off the bus."'

'What had he done wrong?' asked Mark.

'Not a lot,' was the short reply. It was left to Garry to tell the story, as Mark recalled, 'This was a club trip to the Middle East for an exhibition match and they didn't really want to go, but the club needed the money. Garry was injured, they'd played on the Saturday and they were travelling down to Heathrow early on the Sunday morning.

'Garry was complaining on the bus about being injured and how he'd recover better by staying at home. Brian could hear these mutterings and went to speak to Garry about it. He agreed it wasn't going to help the injury.'

The result was that Brian asked Albert the coach driver to stop the bus on Wilford Lane, just a few minutes away from the City Ground. 'They got Garry's suitcase from the back. Clough flagged down a passing motorist and told him to take Garry back to the City Ground.'

Garry told the programme, 'I was injured at the time – surprise, surprise – and I was being taken halfway round the world, as I thought, to a game I couldn't play in. I thought I'd be better staying at Forest, getting treatment from the physio and getting myself fit.

'I was mumbling and grumbling at the back of the coach when the Gaffer got on and said his customary "good mornings" to everybody. He could hear me moaning and he said, "Right, out with it, Gaz. What's wrong?" I explained and he said, "Son, you're right." He told Albert to stop the bus on Wilford Lane and stopped a car coming in the other direction and said, "Can you take Gaz back to the City Ground – he's not coming with us."'

In his book *My Magic Carpet Ride*, Garry said, 'The Gaffer jumped off the bus and was in the middle of the road on the opposite side. He stopped the first car heading in the opposite direction and some poor old guy, who was probably on his way to church, had to slam on the brakes.' The injured striker's bag was put in the surprised motorist's boot and he was taken back to the City Ground.

The irony of the story was the trip to the Middle East didn't go ahead. The flight from Heathrow was aborted after an attempted take-off. Clough, a nervous flyer, marched the team off the plane and they all came back that night.

* * *

When Alan in Woodthorpe called, Forest's neighbours at Meadow Lane were the subject. 'I've been a Notts County supporter for well over 50 years,' was Alan's opening line, before Brian quickly cut in, like a striker pouncing to score a goal, 'Well, I'm sorry about that. You sound as if you have.'

'I'm proud of it,' replied Alan, before asking his question, 'What would have happened if you'd have come to Notts County instead of Forest? Could you have done the same for Notts as you did for Forest?'

It was one of those questions to which no one really knows the answer, including Cloughie. 'Well, you never know, it's a hypothetical question,' came the response.

'I could have done a little bit better or a little bit worse. All I know is they would have got what fraction of expertise I've got as a manager of football.'

What was that? Brian Clough being modest about his abilities as a manager? It was a quality which would surface again when Mark asked him about his achievements. But for now he was happy to praise the Notts County chairman, Derek Pavis, and his board for making him feel welcome at Meadow Lane.

'Since I retired, I've been at Notts County's ground more than I've been at the City Ground. And the supporters have said, "nice to see you at a good ground" – not many have said, "There's Big 'Ead Cloughie."'

The call ended in a kind of harmony which had not been on the cards with those opening words.

Alan bid farewell by adding, 'We only wish you'd have come over to our side and done something for us.'

* * *

The phone-in was broadcast at a time when it wasn't unusual for a BBC local radio presenter/reporter to wear a tie. As a journalist in the newsroom, I would usually wear a suit and tie in those days. My theory was that you never knew who you might be interviewing next and it was important to create a good impression.

Although times changed, with the open-neck shirt becoming more popular, Mark will be forever grateful he wore a smart tie on the day he hosted this phone-in with Cloughie.

The BBC building in Nottingham, where the phone-in was hosted, housed both the local radio and regional TV output of the corporation. Naturally, our television colleagues also wanted a piece of the action when Cloughie arrived.

The only problem was that Brian wasn't wearing a tie and he wanted to look smart if he was to appear on TV. That's where Mark's tie came into the picture.

'Brian wore my tie for the television interview and I let him keep it, as a gift,' said Mark.

As well as giving Cloughie some valuable neck material, he also used it for some lovely comedy material.

'Once he'd got a little nugget like that in his head, he didn't forget it,' added Mark. 'He took quite a shine to this tie.'

During the programme, Mark asked, 'Brian, you were the leading manager at the time, what was it that set you apart from the other managers? What's that special bit that makes you … the legend?'

BC, 'Well, it's difficult to talk about yourself for a start.'

MS, 'I know you're not modest.'

BC, 'Well, I'm not too shy. Having worn your tie before this programme started, I'll never be shy again.'

Clough then explained how he kept his instructions clear and simple: get the ball, keep it and pass it to a colleague.

Surely there was more to it than that? Knowing the answer already, Mark asked what role psychologists, dieticians and fitness coaches had played in the 1970s and early 1980s.

'We regarded European competitions as a holiday,' said Brian. 'The fitness was fine, the beaches were beautiful. The lads were well fed and well looked after. A change of faces. Hey, to get rid of me for two days was the biggest boost I could give them.'

'What about the dieticians and the psychologists?' asked Mark.

'Psychologists?' repeated Cloughie, before launching into a story about one of his Derby players, Ron Webster, enjoying the food during a trip abroad.

'He came and said, "Gaffer, can I have another crab?" I told him, "You've already had two!" And these crabs were the biggest you've ever seen in your life. Anyway, he had another crab. If he'd have wanted another three, I'd have got three for him. We were there to relax and for me to get off their backs.

'It was all about a change of venue and going out to beat the opposition. We wanted to be in that frame of mind. I kept them away from a football. They didn't know what a football was until they kicked off.'

That was football management, Cloughie style.

* * *

Other than describing the incident involving the team bus on the way to Heathrow, Garry Birtles hardly got a word in throughout the programme. He was sitting to the left of Brian but was quite content to let his former boss steal the show. At one point in the proceedings Mark announced, 'You're listening to the Brian Clough Show.' We wouldn't have expected anything else.

Looking back, Mark appreciates how lucky he was to host this historic programme. 'Brian was on top form that night,' he told me. 'He wasn't at his best health-wise but he enjoyed being in the public eye and talking to his fans – his people.'

Although he doesn't like using the word 'ordinary', Mark said Clough was always at his best talking directly with the 'ordinary person' – and that's what the phone-in was all about, 'He wasn't talking to journalists, he was speaking face-to-face, or in this case voice-to-voice, with his fans.'

Those fans included Diane in Radford, who sounded ecstatic to have the opportunity to speak to Brian. With the Miracle Manager in a mischievous mood, their conversation became a 'must-listen' moment.

'Hello Brian, I'm excited,' began Diane, sounding flustered and slightly out of breath.

'Are you married?' asked Brian, as if working up to the punchline. Diane confirmed she was married.

'Well, don't tell your husband you've been talking to me and getting excited,' said Brian. 'I want no problems with you, Diane,' he added with a smile in his voice.

Diane continued, 'I wanted to tell you how wonderful you are – and what I've done today.'

'That's extremely kind,' replied Brian.

Diane explained she had been to the City Ground earlier that day to deliver a petition calling on the club to keep Mark Crossley. Clough had given Crossley his debut in October 1988 – waiting to tell him shortly before the home match against Liverpool that he was playing. Forest won 2-1 and Clough ensured that Crossley was given the match ball – an item he has cherished ever since. These days he still talks of Clough's 'magical management skills'. But in May 2000 Crossley was not being offered a new contract under the management of David Platt.

'I hope he stays,' said Brian, who had worn his famous green sweater at Crossley's recent testimonial match. He still had a soft spot for the goalkeeper as he turned the conversation into a gentle joke at Crossley's expense. Brian said he felt sorry for Crossley's wife – having to see his face every day. 'That must be terrible, because Barbara has the same problem with me,' he added, while also telling Mark not to interrupt him. He was warming up for another story. 'I've got a beautiful wife, she's absolutely gorgeous,' said Brian.

'You're a lucky man, then,' commented Diane, before adding, 'Barbara's very lucky as well.'

'Ah well, she could have done better,' said Brian. 'Academically, she's streets ahead of me. She invented charm. She's fragrant and beautiful, a bit pernickety on occasions when we go out … because I tend to start talking like I am now and everybody's bored to tears with me talking. Anyway, she's absolutely beautiful.'

It was all leading to the punchline, 'She landed on her feet when she met me.'

Back on the subject of Mark Crossley's future, Brian was adamant. 'I think he should be there [at Forest],' he continued. 'The problem is, if you let players go, you've got to replace them with better ones. If a player doesn't want to leave the club, then you should break your neck to keep him there.'

He told the phone-in that throughout his managerial career he had built sides on a solid spine: goalkeeper, centre-half and centre-forward. But finding someone who could be a regular goalscorer was probably the most difficult job.

'You need someone to put it in the back of the net,' said Brian, who reminded listeners he'd been a centre-forward himself, with an outstanding scoring record. 'Believe it or not, I used to score some goals. I got about 270 goals in 250 league games.' There was a pause.

'I had a bad week if I didn't get three,' he said, with the immaculate timing of a comedian.

Mark continued the theme and said that a goalscorer was a priceless commodity.

'It always has been,' said Brian. 'People think it's easy scoring goals. Now, you name me a supporter who comes out of a football match – irrespective of whether there's 60,000 or 16 there – who doesn't say, "He should've scored?"

'It's hard to put one in the back of the net. It's the hardest thing in the world to score a goal – that's why so many get missed.'

That's an assessment which is as true today as it was when Brian uttered those words at the start of the new century.

* * *

Towards the end of the programme, Clough hinted that he'd enjoyed the experience so much that he hoped to return. 'I'm out of work at the moment because I'm retired. Now, I'm going to work on the guy who runs BBC Radio Nottingham and I'm going to go on the salary. It could be only £5 a week – and I'll put my lot in for an hour. But it'll cost five quid because petrol has gone up and I live in Derby.' That sounded a fair enough deal to me.

Mark followed up Cloughie's offer straightaway, 'Unfortunately, we're out of time. But I think Brian was hinting that he might be coming back.' With a smile, and referring to Garry Birtles, Mark added bravely, 'And maybe next time you'll let the man on your left have a quick word.'

'Well, you're in charge,' replied Brian without hesitation. 'All you've got to say is, "Cloughie – shut-up."' Can you imagine? A radio host telling his star guest to be quiet? Brian was playing to the crowd (the listeners) again and came out on top.

At which point, Mark closed proceedings in time for the news bulletin, 'Brian Clough, thank you. It's been a really special one hour on BBC Radio Nottingham. We've had messages, Brian, from people – not just football fans – who've really enjoyed listening to you during the many years you've been associated with Nottingham Forest.'

Following the success of the BBC Radio Nottingham phone-ins (including the one with Brian), Garry Birtles joined the regional commercial station 106 Century FM as the regular guest on its evening phone-in hosted by Darren Fletcher. They formed a formidable and entertaining team and were sometimes joined by Cloughie.

2

Call Cloughie

When a phone-in caller was given the chance to speak directly to Brian Clough and ask about the invaluable support of his wife Barbara, the response was swift and cheeky. 'Do you know her?' enquired Cloughie. Before there was a chance for a reply, the follow-up comment was a typical moment of mischievous humour, 'It's not you who's seeing her behind my back, is it?'

As the BBC had discovered in May 2000, it was always wise to expect the unexpected when Brian was invited to take part in a live radio phone-in programme. Thankfully, it was a situation that presenter Darren Fletcher handled admirably when Brian began a regular show on commercial radio in the East Midlands.

Often accompanied by Garry Birtles, who had helped to organise Brian's appearance on that first phone-in on BBC Radio Nottingham, *Call Cloughie* became a monthly appointment-to-listen on the East Midlands station, 106 Century FM. On other occasions, right up to 2004, he was sometimes joined by his son Nigel or the ex-Forest defender Kenny Burns (or 'Kenneth' as Brian called him).

Listening back to some of these old recordings I'd collected, and kept for many years in my loft on cassettes or mini-discs, it was just like stepping back into a golden age when Brian could 'hold court' for 20 minutes at a time (in between the adverts). He would regale stories from the glory days at Derby and Forest, as well giving his 'no holds barred' opinions on issues which remain relevant in modern-day football.

Fans would call in not knowing what to expect, as entertainingly demonstrated in the case of the supporter who asked about Barbara. On that occasion it led to a story about the time Brian was still playing football and visited Russia as part of the England squad. 'She's a cracker,' he said of Barbara. 'She's the exact opposite to me.' Brian said Mrs Clough enjoyed going to the theatre and was excellent at TV quizzes – the types of things that bored the pants off him, 'She never forgave me when I was playing with the England side and they took us to the Bolshoi Ballet and she said it was a complete waste on people like me. And it was, actually. They were doing the dying swan and, if you know ballet at all, the lady falls down right at the end of the job.' Note the reference to 'the job', indicating it was something he could easily take or leave. Well, perhaps preferably leave altogether, as the remainder of the story showed. He proceeded to describe what happened next to the ballet dancer, 'She went down about three times and she kept getting up. I said to Bobby Charlton, who was sitting next to me, "If she gets up once more, *I'll* shoot her!"' There was spontaneous laughter in the studio. But Cloughie wasn't finished. 'And then an official from the FA got on to me and said, "Brian, you don't say things like that about the ballet."' Maybe that's an early indication of the Football Association's reservations about the type of thing Clough would say in public, if he had ever been made England manager.

* * *

My dad was lucky enough to have not one, but two phone conversations with Cloughie – both instigated by me. I've already outlined the first call in the previous chapter. The second occasion came along less than a year later. It was another case of 'Mission Dad' as he called in to another phone-in on my behalf. At the time, I was working for the BBC and I'd have got into all kinds of trouble if I'd contacted a rival station's phone-in to ask a question. So when I heard that Brian and Nigel were appearing on *Call Cloughie* in January 2001, 'Mission Dad' was launched.

Don't get me wrong, it was nothing underhand, I wasn't trying to catch anyone out or 'hijack' a live phone-in. Far from it. The reason that I was keen to ask Cloughie a question – a genuine question – was because I'd recently launched the not-for-profit tribute website, brianclough.com, and I wanted to know what he thought about the idea. Although I'd written to him before the website went live, to check he didn't have a problem with the online tribute, I'd not received a reply at that stage. Listening back to the conversation between Dad and Brian – a recording I'd not played for 20-odd years – was a special moment for me.

'David, good evening to you,' began Brian, when Dad was put through to talk to him, live on the radio show.

'How are you?' asked Dad.

'Not bad at all, thanks son,' came the reply. All was sounding good so far. The pleasantries were out of the way and now Dad could focus on the job at hand. He explained there had been a report on the radio about a website that had been set up in tribute to Brian and asked whether he'd heard about it, what he thought in general to the idea and whether he'd logged on himself.

'Well, I didn't hear it for a start,' he said. 'I think it's a good idea, simple as that. And if he's picked me to do one [a website], then why not?'

That was the endorsement I was hoping for. But Dad didn't leave it there. He went on to explain how the website had been created by a Cloughie fan and that other fans could use it to write their own tributes and memories. At that point, the call was quickly ended due to concern that it was a free advert. Fortunately, Nigel eased the situation by quickly commenting, 'He's talking to the wrong people about websites.' That prompted laughter in the studio. Bear in mind that when the *Middlesbrough Gazette* newspaper had asked Nigel about the launch of the website, he said his dad wouldn't have known a computer if it bit him! But he added that no one had a problem with the website being set up.

Personally, I was just relieved that Brian himself had said publicly that he thought this special online tribute was a good idea. Anyone who had listened to Century would have known that the site was not a commercial enterprise, because I'd been interviewed by their news team specifically about its launch, with the BBC's permission. They'd used soundbites of me on their news bulletins. I'd explained that it was purely a hobby and that, far from it being a money-making outlet, the website was actually costing me money to set up and run (this was in the very early days of web hosting and dial-up internet).

Over the years, the website became a focal point for people around the world to send their tributes, 'get well' messages and support for the knighthood campaign which I launched. I made a point of printing out all the lovely messages after Brian's liver transplant and delivering them personally to his home. All that is explained in my first book, *Young Man, You've Made My Day*, which raised money for charity. It also tells the story of how the website was a driving force behind the fundraising campaign I instigated for the Clough statue in Nottingham. The small group of volunteers that I gathered together came up with many imaginative ideas, leading to the target of £70,000 being smashed within 18 months – long before the days of online fundraising sites. We worked tirelessly, with Cloughie's family, the city council and Nottingham Forest, to make it happen. At the time, Forest said there were no plans for a statue at the City Ground. Following the unveiling of the sculpture by Barbara Clough in 2008, it remains a huge source of pride for everyone involved – especially when you see visitors from around the world still having selfies with it. Anyway, you get the idea. The website has always been a labour of love, which helps to raise money for good causes.

Going back to the phone-in, Dad's call had put my mind at rest. Cloughie had given his approval, his famous thumbs-up if you like. And the recording is very special too. Dad passed away in 2016 and I think about him every day. We would often chat on the phone about football, including memories of Cloughie. Having that recording of his voice remains something to cherish.

* * *

During the phone-in with Nigel at his side, Brian revealed how he felt 'ashamed' by Forest's relegation during his final season at the club. He was responding to a caller who asked whether, with hindsight, he would have bought the striker Stan Collymore to keep Forest up. The answer was an emphatic no.

'I stuck with what I thought would get us through. We didn't get through and it cost me my resignation. I might have hung on if we'd have stayed up,' said Cloughie. 'I was a bit ashamed we got relegated. I didn't think we could because we had such a good lot of players. I know I had bad luck with Pearcey [Stuart Pearce] and Webbie [Neil Webb] and a few players. I still didn't think we could get relegated and I was a bit ashamed we did.'

Another listener asked the Master Manager whether, looking back, he would have handled things differently at Derby County after resigning following a row with the directors. Clough said, with hindsight, he wouldn't have let such a disagreement with directors force him out, 'I shouldn't have left Derby. That was the biggest mistake I made. I had a side at Derby that would have gone on to compete with, and better, Liverpool. Liverpool were the kings of the castle at that time.'

In another personal appearance in 2002, he reflected again on his departure from Derby and concluded that everyone in life had regrets. 'Edith Piaf used to sing about regrets,' he said. 'Of course, I had regrets about leaving. It's one of the mistakes in life. Conceit probably made me finish in the first place – the fact I thought I was the 'bee's knees' and I wasn't. It's inevitable that it goes through your mind and your dreams.'

At that same event, he was asked how he felt about both Forest and Derby no longer being in the top flight at the time. 'I'm genuinely sorry to see Derby and Forest where they are now,' he said. 'I feel it's self-inflicted. You're both in the position of having no money. These days, money is absolutely essential in modern-day football.' He then used the examples of some of his former players to illustrate the importance of finding talent without spending a fortune, 'There are no David Mackays hanging around now and coming to play for buttons. There are no Roy McFarlands coming for £20,000 and no John Robertsons who cost nothing. I signed Roger Davies for two lorry loads of plums.' At that point there was a huge roar of laughter from the audience who had come to see him. 'He came from Worcester – good plum-growing territory. So it was part of the deal.'

* * *

Many of the callers to the phone-ins simply wanted to thank Old Big 'Ead for the enjoyment he had provided over the years. The reply was usually met with a little comical modesty, 'That's extremely kind. I know you're fibbing, now get on with your question …'

On other occasions, he would pull-up the caller for not using their correct name. In the same way he referred to 'Kenneth Burns' rather than 'Kenny', he would make a point of using the full names of those who phoned in.

Nick from Stapleford was introduced and asked Brian how good he thought Sir Alex Ferguson was as a manager.

'It's Nicholas, isn't it? You were christened Nicholas.'

'Yes, that's right.' Well, you're hardly going to argue with Cloughie, are you?

'Obviously, he's a good manager,' said Brian, quickly moving the conversation on to one of his favourite subjects. 'Manchester United have for years been the biggest club in Europe. Alex Ferguson has been there long enough to get to a point where they're dominating nearly everything. So, you've got to give him credit.

'When he first went there, he had a terrible time, and the few times he and I talked he was down in the dumps, he was having problems managing such a big club. Actually, we got him out of the cart because he came to Nottingham Forest and beat us in the FA Cup and that set him going and kept him in a job. But he's come through it. I hope his eyesight improves this season, because every time he's asked if a Manchester United player has committed a sin, he says, "I didn't see it!"'

During one of the programmes, Brian also spoke for the first time about his nomination for a knighthood (the campaign I had started). This time, I didn't need to launch 'Mission Dad.' Instead, a caller asked whether he had known anything about the nomination.

'I know as much as you, actually,' said Clough. 'I didn't know whether it was true or not.'

And he joked about who was responsible for putting his name forward, 'I thought it was my next door neighbour because I think she felt if I got something like that, I'd have to move.'

During another programme, Brian was asked whether he would like to receive the honour. He replied, 'It would be tremendous. But I don't decide things like that. I decide where our Queen lives and how much money we give her and mundane things like that. But I don't decide knighthoods.'

I've been asked several times over the years whether Brian would have accepted a knighthood. That answer alone gives a clear indication. When I spoke to his friend Colin Shields some years later, he also confirmed to me that Brian would have accepted the honour – more to recognise the amazing support of his wife Barbara than for himself.

When the subject of a knighthood came up, the phone-in host Darren Fletcher was spot-on when he put it to Clough that he deserved the honour just as much as Sir Alex Ferguson.

'That's extremely kind,' replied Brian. 'He had a slight head start. He is manager of the biggest club in Europe. He has got everything at his fingertips.

'We went to Old Trafford and had our fair share of wins and they were not playing to their full potential. Now he has got it right and his signings have come off. Young players have come through, which is inevitable.'

Clough said that many youngsters, when asked, would say they wanted to play for Manchester United. 'That's a hell of a start,' he said. And showing his unique managerial style, he added, 'I used to have to buy fish and chips at 11 o'clock for the parents of youngsters we signed. I have eaten chips walking along the street with the parents of kids we wanted.'

Brian also liked to have a joke at Sir Alex Ferguson's expense. He recalled having a drink with the Manchester United manager before a match, 'He took me into his office and gave me a drop of sherry. I told him I didn't think they were still making thimbles.'

When it was suggested that the Old Trafford boss would always face considerable pressure, Brian replied that the situation was no different to how it was some 15 years previously. Pressure went with the territory, he said. Warming to the topic, Clough added that it was rubbish to suggest that, because Nottingham Forest were considered a small club at the time, he had not felt any pressure.

'We got as much pressure as anybody got, as much as Manchester United – and they were the biggest club in Europe for donkeys' years. We never spent £18m on two teams, let alone on one player.' Brian said it was ironic to see United sitting seventh or eighth in the league, as they were at the time of that particular phone-in. 'We all have a little grin to ourselves,' he said cheekily. 'I am bl***y delighted, absolutely delighted. And it's not being nasty or anything like that, because it's part and parcel of the nature of this country that we soon get sick of people winning everything. It's a lovely feeling to see somebody come from the lower end of the league and put one over the big boys.'

Alison in Heanor asked Brian what he thought about the spate of bookings and sendings-off among players at one of his former clubs. It was another of his favourite subjects. Not only was he disappointed with the lack of discipline on the field, but he pointed the finger at what he described as, 'bad management'. Managers were responsible for the way players performed, he said. 'If the system understands that managers will be fined for the misdemeanours of the players on the pitch, the managers will soon cut it out,' he explained. 'If they don't cut it out, the directors will cut the managers out. It's got to improve.'

* * *

Listening back to these programmes was like wandering into a special corner of history. I'm so glad I kept these recordings of a football genius giving his honest and hugely entertaining opinions, many of which are still relevant today. The quality of the recordings is by no means perfect – some were made by placing a microphone next to a car radio speaker because it wasn't always easy to get a good radio signal at home. Several were recorded on to cassette by my father-in-law Roland when I was busy at work. Yet at a time, now, when many managers produce the same tired quotes, and quality pundits are a precious and rare commodity, these tapes simply confirm – if any confirmation was needed – how much I miss hearing Cloughie's colourful views, on everything from on-field discipline to signing players for a packet of fish and chips, or a lorry load of plums.

When one of the programmes had finished and Brian had left the building, Darren Fletcher hit the nail on the head when he told listeners, 'It was a privilege to be in the same room and listen to what he had to say. If anybody needed any proof that man is as sharp as a razor, we've just had it.

'We were fortunate to sit down with him for half an hour before the show started and just talk football. And I tell you what, what he has forgotten about football other people don't know yet.'

3

Trophy Room

The lights of the film crew were shining on the trophies. Sitting alongside them, with the European Cup in prime position, was the man who'd been the mastermind behind the incredible collection of silverware. Smartly dressed in a suit and tie, Cloughie sat back and enjoyed telling some of the stories from his amazing managerial career. He was being interviewed by the TV sports presenter Keith Daniell for a special project to mark the 25th anniversary of the European Cup success at Nottingham Forest.

Using some vivid imagery to describe how he unearthed gem-like players and coaxed-out their incredible skills, Clough explained some of the secrets of his success, 'There's no point in having a diamond, 40ft down, if nobody knows it's there. When you dig them up, they're covered in dirt and they've got to be polished and shaped and shorn, and given the right light – and then they glimmer and they sparkle. John Robertson was in that category – so was Martin O'Neill – and all the players I never get tired of talking about. So, forgive me if I rant and rave, but when you've come across something in life that good and that delicate, and that bright and beautiful, it does stick in your brain, if you've got one.'

For Keith Daniell, the half-hour interview was one of the highlights of his career. 'It was absolutely awe-inspiring for me to be in the trophy room and interview him there,' said Keith. 'To be with him, with all that silverware … was a huge part of my career and a privilege. Let's be honest, I would have paid to do that – and actually I was *getting* paid to do it.'

Like many Clough interviews, there was the sense that you never quite knew what was coming next. 'I think anybody who ever interviewed Brian would say there was always that slight element of unpredictability with him,' said Keith. 'You were never quite sure what you were going to get.'

Fortunately for Keith, he was able to record some wonderful comments that were as gem-like as the diamonds Cloughie spoke about. 'All this business about "they played with fear", and they were frightened of me – what a load of rubbish,' insisted Brian as he talked about accusations that his players were fearful of him. 'The only time they were frightened of me was if they went to bed early on a Thursday or Friday and I had to get them out to have a glass of champagne. And we did that a few times.'

Cloughie explained that having a good meal and something to drink helped the players relax, 'It's one of the things that affects teams, they can't sleep before a match. Our lads slept like logs.' That was especially important before away matches, when he would ensure the team was in a relaxed frame of mind once they were at the hotel. They would have something to drink: tea, coffee or a glass of bubbly. 'We'd sit around for an hour, then up to bed and slept like logs for nine hours. And we'd take *anybody* on after that. After two glasses of champagne, we'd have played them on *Friday* night, never mind Saturday.' Keith couldn't resist chuckling as Brian finished his answer with a cheeky smile.

Long before the concept of media training and the idea of producing soundbites became popular, Clough was already the master of it. 'He was brilliant at that,' said Keith. 'Whatever you asked him, he would answer it brilliantly but, a bit like a politician, he could tell you what he wanted to say even if it wasn't quite the answer to the question you'd asked. But he had that ability to communicate with people on any level and could reach out and press the buttons that would motivate people.'

Another method for preparing for tense matches was to take the players away for a change of scene. Cloughie described to Keith how he would treat European Cup away games as a holiday. 'I used to tell them, "We're going away to do nowt,"' recalled Brian. Famously, before the second European Cup Final, the Forest players were taken to one of Cloughie's favourite places for relaxation, Calor Millor on Majorca's east coast. It was a chance for them all to get a bit of sunshine on their backs, 'We didn't train a lot,' added Brian. 'We went for five days and we just relaxed and had a good time. They [the players] would ask me, "Can we do a bit of training?" And I'd say, "Yes, you can run up that beach and run back again."'

During the title-winning season, a trip to Benidorm followed an emphatic 4-0 win over Manchester United. John Robertson recalled having 'a great time', especially when 'Mull of Kintyre' was played in a pub there called the Robin Hood. The song was number one in the charts and is still the adopted anthem among Reds fans. Robbo said that when the record by Paul McCartney and

Wings was played over the speakers in the bar, 'John O'Hare used to grab a snorkel that was positioned behind the bar and pretend it was the bagpipes.' He said it was so funny that his team-mates encouraged him to repeat the performance every time the song was played in the pub.

But not all the excursions were universally popular with the players. Ian Bowyer told me about a trip to Jersey that didn't go down well with many of the Forest squad back in 1980. 'It was the longest trip ever, it was a drag,' he recalled. 'And because of the result that followed, it became the worst trip ever.'

Shortly after returning from Jersey, the Reds lost the League Cup Final against Wolves. The trip (illustrated in this book, thanks to the *Jersey Evening Post*) left the players in the wrong frame of mind. 'I remember it distinctly because it was the week that Cheltenham Races were on,' said Bowyer. 'Footballers being footballers, we wanted to sit in front of the television and watch Cheltenham Races. But with Peter [Taylor] and Brian, we ended up going here, there and everywhere. We were proper tourists. I think it's fair to say we didn't enjoy it too much.'

But generally speaking, the sunshine breaks were a welcome diversion during a gruelling season. Reflecting on those trips abroad, during a 2001 recording I listened to on a cassette tape, Brian said he took the players away at a time when many observers thought the idea was 'crackers'. It was important, he said, to relax and recuperate in order to perform at your very best.

'To win a league championship, you've got to battle,' he stressed. 'And then to win a European Cup, you've got to battle. You've got to play a lot of games – and a lot of high-tension games – against a lot of good players. So every opportunity I had, I used to take the players away. It built team spirit.' And that camaraderie should never be underestimated. It wasn't simply a foreign jaunt for the sake of it, as he explained in his closing remark, 'I did it with every club. It built up this spirit which got us through many, many times when we shouldn't have got through.'

With a small squad and a relentless fixture list, these trips to enjoy the sunshine were usually squeezed in between league matches. There's no surprise, then, that Brian supported the idea of a mid-season break. He was asked about it in another recording, from March 2004, and pointed out that his long-time assistant, Peter Taylor, had extolled the virtues of such a break some 35 years previously. 'He said, "Don't you fancy a couple of weeks in May and June playing football with everybody in short-sleeve shirts and shorts, and a lovely atmosphere, instead of January and February?"' Cloughie said it was a good idea and that the introduction of a fixture break halfway through the season was inevitable. Having suffered an injury which effectively ended his playing career on a cold Boxing Day afternoon, he added, 'I don't want anybody to play on an icy, thick, dirty, stinking pitch I was playing on the day I got injured.'

Picture the scene. Two of Brian Clough's European Cup heroes are pacing up and down, nervously waiting for the arrival of their former boss, who had recently retired. Even though Cloughie was no longer their manager, there was an air of apprehension as the film crew waited in Martin O'Neill's office at Leicester City, where he and John Robertson were in charge. The meeting was Keith Daniell's idea. Keith explained to me how this reunion came about, 'Brian had actually been retired for a year or more and I had this idea for ITV that we'd take him out of retirement and make him the interviewer.' The plan was for Clough to meet up with former players and managers. 'I wasn't sure how Brian would get on as an interviewer,' said Keith, 'but I should never have had any doubts because he was brilliant. The interviewees had respect for him and they wanted to be part of it.'

For Keith, the most memorable encounter was Clough's meeting with O'Neill and Robertson, 'It was just before they left Leicester City and they were absolutely flying high. We set up in Martin's office and waited for Brian to arrive. Now, you've got to remember you'd got two people here – in Martin O'Neill and John Robertson – who have won the European Cup and are the hottest managers around at the time. Grown men, incredibly confident, and yet they were waiting for their former boss, Brian, to come down and interview them. Robbo was like a cat on a hot tin roof, pacing up and down. He kept asking, "When's the boss going to arrive? When's the boss coming?" And Martin was on tenterhooks too. It was extraordinary. They were like kids outside the headmaster's room waiting to be told off.'

When Brian arrived and the interview began, it was only a matter of moments before O'Neill brought up the issue of his controversial omission from the team that played in the 1979 European Cup Final. All those years later, O'Neill still wanted to make the point that he had been ready to play against Malmö and had recovered from injury. 'For the first few minutes, Martin went on, exorcising these demons from the fact that Brian had made the decision to leave him out,' recalled Keith. 'It was incredible. Brian didn't get a word in for the first ten minutes of the interview.' Now, that must have been a first! Interestingly, in an interview with Adrian Chiles on BBC Radio 5 Live, O'Neill said he now understood why Clough had left him out. It was November 2022 and O'Neill was talking about his excellent book *On Days Like These*. He admitted he could understand the manager's decision to not risk a player who had been injured, 'I couldn't see that as a player, I wanted to play in a European Cup Final. But now I see the managerial viewpoint.'

During Keith's interview with Brian in the Nottingham Forest trophy room, Cloughie spoke fondly about O'Neill, a player he regularly had arguments with in the dressing room. He said the greatest compliment O'Neill had paid him was when they were together for that reunion in the manager's office at Leicester. O'Neill said he never understood one of the boss's instructions: stop the cross. For two years, those words had left him confused. 'I told him, "That's coaching,"' said Brian. If the ball was stopped from being crossed into the penalty area, the chances were that the opposition wouldn't score. 'It's as simple as A-B-C to me,' said Clough, who showed that when it came to football qualifications, simplicity scored top marks. 'He's a tremendous manager and a tremendous young man who'll go from strength to strength,' added Brian.

In an interview with Garry Richardson on BBC Radio 4's *Today* programme in November 2022, O'Neill explained that a lot of Clough's coaching was conducted *during* games rather than before them. 'Lots of people thought he was a fantastic motivator and may be not so big on the tactics – and that's probably true, he wasn't,' said O'Neill. 'However, [with] some of his points, he didn't spend time on the training ground telling you about these things. He told you at the most important time – during the matches, when you would never forget. He knew the game inside out.'

However, one particular incident that O'Neill would never forget during a match was when Cloughie substituted him at Wembley, even though he was close to scoring a hat-trick. Clough seemed almost apologetic as he told Keith Daniell what happened. 'I must tell you about the terrible things I did to the poor lad,' said Brian, who explained that O'Neill never forgave him for two incidents: leaving him out of the team for the 1979 European Cup Final and substituting him when he was on a hat-trick in the Charity Shield match against Ipswich. Of the latter, Clough said Forest were leading 4-1, including two goals from O'Neill, when he turned to coach Jimmy Gordon and said, 'Get him off.' When Gordon questioned the decision, pointing out that O'Neill was on two goals and close to scoring a hat-trick, the response was abrupt, 'I don't care if he's got 22. Get him off!' Gordon asked why the midfielder was being substituted. 'We need two footballs out there – one for Martin and one for the other ten, because he's trying to get a hat-trick,' came the response. Clough added that when O'Neill came off, he thought he would get a tracksuit top flung in his face. Of course, no one was brave enough to do that.

'But we've retained a friendship and it's grown over the years,' reflected Clough. 'Respect from me to him has grown – and from him to me.'

That admiration was clear when Brian spoke in glowing terms about his former player during a radio show, 'If he'd been English, he'd have got the England job.

He'd have got it before the Swede who got it.' Clough was referring to Sven-Göran Eriksson who became England boss in 2001. Brian went on to say he was pleased that O'Neill had retained his charm and enthusiasm.

Another thing that hadn't changed, he said, was O'Neill's passion for talking, 'I'm telling you, when I first came to Nottingham Forest, he was chuntering on and every time I dropped him – which I think was every other week – he chuntered on. He gave me the same line every week, "Oh, I might as well be at university doing history and maths." Intellectually, he's quite bright. Bear in mind that I came from a secondary modern and when I throw my qualifications on the table, I throw European Cup medals on. I can't throw many A-Levels. But my A-Levels are European Cups. So, I stood this for about a month and I got that sick of it that I told him, "Martin, if you mention that once more, I'll personally *book* you a place at university!"'

In his interview with Keith, Brian referred to being so fed up with O'Neill complaining that on one occasion he reached into his breast pocket and produced a fake airline ticket to Belfast. He then showed it to the midfielder. 'I'd got a dummy ticket made, so I told him, "If you want to go, here you are."' When I asked O'Neill about this, he said that although he couldn't remember Clough presenting him with a dummy ticket, the sentiment was spot-on.

* * *

For the final programme of Keith's series of TV features, Cloughie was taken to a school to become the manager of a team of 11-year-olds. 'Slightly to my surprise, he agreed to it,' recalled Keith. 'On the day we did the filming, it was freezing cold, a horrible day and the rain was chucking it down. Brian turned up and I had this idea that I'd start it by taking him into the classroom to meet the children and answer their questions.'

Before he met the youngsters, Brian asked who the captain of the team was. It turned out it was a lad called Aaron. 'Brian said, "Right, *he* gets the first question."' The children were all sitting on the floor. Although, ordinarily, they may not have known who Brian was, a letter about Clough's visit had been sent to their homes the day before, so their parents would probably have explained exactly who their special visitor was. Aaron's question was simple but important, 'Mr Clough, when we get out there this afternoon, what should we do?'

Brian reached into his pocket and produced a tennis ball. He was fully prepared for a coaching session, Clough style. 'If I throw this tennis ball to you, Aaron, what will you do?' The team captain said he would catch it. Brian threw him the ball and Aaron duly caught it.

'What are you going to do with it now, Aaron?' The young lad looked around his schoolmates and replied that he would throw it to his friend, Emily. 'Go on, then,' encouraged Brian, who proceeded to watch the ball being carefully caught by Emily.

'What are *you* going to do with it?' Brian asked. 'I'm going to throw it to Sarah,' replied Emily – and that's exactly what she did. 'Right, now you throw it back to me,' instructed Brian, who caught the tennis ball. 'Now that's all you do,' he said. 'When you get out there this afternoon, you get hold of the ball, you look after it, you give it to your friend, they look after it and they give it to a friend. And if you get anywhere near the goal, you just kick it at the goal.'

It was the type of team talk that had brought unprecedented success over the previous decades. Here was the Master Manager passing on his advice to a team of eager young players. And he hadn't finished there. 'But don't give it away,' he told them. 'Don't lose it. Look after it as if it's your friend.' Trophy-winning teams who had lifted major silverware in the professional game had heard the same instructions down the years. Keith witnessed this classroom team talk, 'I just thought it was the best, simple explanation. Brilliant.'

Standing on the touchline that afternoon, watching the youngsters playing football, Clough was as unpredictable as ever. As a former centre-forward, he kept an eye on his team's own centre-forward, who began getting closer to the halfway line, instead of the opposing goal. 'This centre-forward kept coming back further and further to get the ball,' said Keith. 'Even though it was a friendly game for a group of youngsters – and he was long retired – he was getting more and more frustrated with this. After about five minutes, that was it.'

'Centre-forward! You're off!' shouted Brian. The young lad was substituted and quickly learned his lesson. After a few minutes, the youngster was brought back on to the pitch and the team continued to play the ball to each other. It didn't matter whether it was a professional team or a school team, the football law according to Clough was just the same: concentrate on doing your own job well. The same treatment was dished out to Duncan McKenzie after he signed for Cloughie at Leeds United. During an interview on talkSPORT in 2011, McKenzie recalled, 'In my first league game, he walked on to the pitch to speak to me. He said, "Young man, I pay you to score goals. You are not going to score them in our half – get out there! You are a liability down there!"'

Back at the school match, Keith said he would never forget watching Clough working with the youngsters that afternoon, demonstrating that – whatever his audience and whoever he was with – he remained a natural and brilliant communicator.

During my chat with Keith, he described another occasion when those same communication skills were on show. Cloughie was receiving the Freedom of Nottingham at the time and spoke to an invited audience in the Ballroom of Nottingham Council House. Keith had conducted an interview with Brian when he arrived and then took his place inside, among many former players and city councillors. He still remembers the impact of the acceptance speech, 'I was never in a dressing room with Brian – apart from being with the kids when he visited the school – but he spoke from the stage for about ten or 15 minutes and he was inspirational. These days I help people to communicate better and you talk to people about rhetoric, using their voice, about pausing, and using light and shade and appropriate gestures. I don't know if Brian ever studied any of this, but on that night, in that room and on that occasion, I would have done anything he'd have asked.

'If he had said, "Go and run through a brick wall," or, "Go and jump off the Council House balcony," I would have done, because he used his voice and imagery. I can only imagine, in a tiny way, what it must have been like when he was absolutely at his prime in a dressing room. In that closed environment, he would have said something that made you feel so important that when you went out there, you would have been unbelievably motivated. At that particular time, he was just so phenomenal that he made you feel you could achieve anything. I think that's one of the great skills he had.'

Those motivational powers in the dressing room were recalled vividly when I interviewed Martin O'Neill. Often at odds with Clough, O'Neill could never understand why he didn't get the same level of praise as his friend and team-mate John Robertson. O'Neill craved Clough's approval, but it wasn't until half-time in the 1980 European Cup Final that he secured the praise he'd been hoping for. Brian was speaking to the players and was thinking about a possible positional tweak within the team for the second half.

'We came in after John Robertson had given us the lead and we were doing fine,' said O'Neill, 'but we knew that Hamburg, with all the players at their disposal, would come at us particularly strongly in the second half to get an equaliser. I think Clough was vectoring to make some sort of positional change at the time. I'm not sure what it was but I semi-volunteered to go into this position that he was looking for. And that's when he said, "No son, you're doing brilliantly where you are." And what a lift that gave you for the second half. Just those words coming from him, like an adrenalin lift coming right through your body again. You're thinking, "Wow, this is great. He actually thinks you're doing really well."'

O'Neill told me how the impact of Clough's message to the team would be delivered largely by the way he spoke. He could have been talking about dog walking and people would listen, enthralled. 'We were looking for that approval from him,' added O'Neill. 'It was as if he was the Godfather of football. He knew everything about the game. He knew us inside out, and you just wanted to sit at his right-hand table.'

4

Microphone Man

Working as a journalist, you never quite know what each day will have in store for you – where you may be sent on a story and who you might meet next. It's also a profession which can open doors that are usually closed for many other people. As a BBC journalist in London, working with a showbusiness brief, I was tasked with reporting the launch of the BBC TV schedule for the autumn.

When I reached Television Centre at White City, I waited in reception for 30 minutes, wondering who would be made available for me to interview for my radio report. The door opened – and to my amazement several stars of the soap *EastEnders*, including Dame Barbara Windsor, were waiting for me. On other occasions, I was given the opportunity to interview the lead singer of Status Quo, Francis Rossi, record producer Pete Waterman and *Strictly Come Dancing* star Anton Du Beke. The disgraced media figures Max Clifford and Jonathan King were also interviewees – but that's for another time!

For my friend Chris Ellis, journalism opened the door of Brian Clough's home in Derby. Not only that, but he found himself kneeling in between Brian and his European Cup-winning captain, John McGovern, as they chatted on the sofa. It sounds a bizarre situation, so let me explain.

The sports team working at the BBC in Nottingham were looking for a fresh approach to previewing a forthcoming derby fixture between Nottingham Forest and Derby County. It was during the time that McGovern was a match summariser for BBC Radio Nottingham. The idea was hatched that John – who was still in touch with his former boss – would interview him. Arrangements were made for John to visit Brian at home and record their conversation. The man given the responsibility of capturing this historic discussion was Chris, then a young freelance journalist.

Chris told me, 'John wasn't technical, he didn't know how to operate a recording machine, so I got the call to help out and go to Cloughie's house to record them. Not many people get that opportunity. It was too good to turn down.

'I can still remember being with John as he strode up confidently to the front door. And there's me, a petrified 20-something, going to Brian Clough's house with him. It was incredible.'

In order to get the best sound quality for the recording, Chris ended up kneeling on the floor while Brian and John chatted on the sofa. 'I had to get in between them somehow to get close enough to record their voices and the only way to do that was to kneel on the floor,' said Chris.

These days, recording devices are extremely compact. In fact, smartphones are often used for some radio interviews, with a suitable broadcast-quality app installed. But back in October 2002, the portable recording machine used by Chris was still quite a chunky piece of equipment.

'The microphone was long and I was moving it between John and Brian, from one way to the other,' recalled Chris. 'One of my lasting memories is that within five minutes my arm was aching so much! I think they spoke for about 20 to 30 minutes, so you can imagine what it was like. I really wanted to stop and have a rest, but you can't tell two of the most famous people in local footballing history to stop while you re-adjust your microphone. The best I could do was change hands a couple of times.'

Before the interview, Brian managed to have a quick look at some of John's notes, which included the reminder to ask about how the match was going to play out – and who was going to win. The Gaffer used the notes to his advantage straightaway, with a humorous start to the conversation.

BC, 'John, good afternoon to you, what can I do for you? You're not going to ask me who's going to win between Forest and Derby?

JM [with a laugh], 'No, I thought you'd get me with that one!'

John then asked whether a team's preparation for a derby match was different to any other game. He recalled that, as a player, there hadn't been a different approach when getting ready for a local derby.

BC, 'Perfectly true … if I could have improved the preparation, I would have done. I used to take great pride and pleasure in sending a side out to be prepared for every match. We found a formula very early on – you couldn't send a team out feeling nervous, for a start.'

JM, 'You had to be relaxed.'

BC, 'Yes, anybody who's nervous in any walk of life cannot perform to the best of their ability. We knew we had the ability, but I didn't want them freezing up in the dressing room and not portraying everything they had.'

John recalled that the preparations under Clough started with training sessions that were as intense as any match. But he also mentioned that training could involve running through a compost heap! 'Garry Birtles didn't like that,' he added, with a smile in his voice. 'I think it was the nettles he didn't like.'

BC, 'Well, I wasn't going to mention the nettles – because they reached a wee bit higher and stung him in a delicate place!'

* * *

John asked Brian how he would have dealt with some of the fashion statements made by a few of the big-name footballers at the time. It seems trivial these days, but even the red hair of Arsenal's Freddie Ljungberg was a talking point then.

Brian said he remembered a Forest player coming into the dressing room sporting a Mohican haircut – with a strip of spiky hair over the centre of his head and shaved at the sides.

'He had a beautiful head of hair when it was done properly,' said Brian. 'So I said to him, "Come here, what the hell are you doing?" And that's mild for me! He said, "Boss, I want to be different." So I said, "Ah, I can make you different, son." He replied, "How can you do that, boss?" I told him, "Get me three goals on Saturday." Martin O'Neill fell on the floor laughing.'

Cloughie's comments about the follicle foibles of some footballers reminded me about his verdict on the former England goalkeeper, David Seaman. It was back in August 2000 and Brian was talking about the importance of having a top-class goalkeeper. He said it was vital to establish a strong spine to any side – and that started with the stopper.

'Many in the game know nowt about the value of a reliable keeper,' he said. 'At Forest, Peter Shilton won me 15 points per season and a couple of European Cups, because he was inspirational.'

Looking at the England goalkeepers available at the time, Brian reckoned that Leeds United's Nigel Martyn was ahead of Seaman in the pecking order. 'That Seaman is a handsome young man,' added Cloughie, 'but he spends too much time looking in his mirror, rather than at the ball. You can't keep goal with hair like that!'

Talking of Shilton, the former TV sports reporter Dennis Coath has worked with the former England goalkeeper on a couple of books and told me that Clough wouldn't have won two European Cups without him.

'Peter Shilton was probably the one player that Cloughie really left alone and was almost in awe of,' said Dennis. 'He let Peter do his own thing because Peter knew exactly what he was doing. He was the exemplary professional. He'd stay behind after training and get the kids to have shooting practice. The other players would be in the changing rooms having a shower and getting changed while Peter would be out there training.'

Like me, Dennis could not understand why the England manager back then, Ron Greenwood, couldn't make his mind up between Shilton and Liverpool's Ray Clemence. Greenwood kept swapping them for each match. 'Ray Clemence was good but Peter Shilton was the best in the world,' added Dennis. 'I found it extraordinary that Ron Greenwood would rotate them.'

When I spoke to Shilton for a video for my Brian Clough tribute website, he said one of the things that he'd always remember about Cloughie was the way he treated everybody the same – from a top player to the 'tea lady'. Funnily enough, the former Fleet Street journalist Norman Giller told me how Brian insisted that Shilton made the tea for a group of journalists when he was introduced as a new signing.

'I remember when he signed Peter Shilton he called five of us into his office,' said Giller. 'Brian told us, "Come and meet the world's greatest goalkeeper." Then he got Peter to make the tea for us – and that included getting the right number of sugars for everyone. He had reduced the world's greatest goalkeeper to a tea boy!'

* * *

Listening back to the conversation between Clough and McGovern, Chris Ellis recalled just how anxious he was when he arrived at Brian's house, 'Brian was very friendly but I was nervous. When I listen to the recording, you can hear at the start that I'm talking to myself, which shows just how nervous I was.'

Like all good interviewers, McGovern was determined to get an answer to the key question: who did Cloughie think would have the bragging rights and be victorious in the forthcoming derby between the Reds and the Rams? 'I remember John trying to tease out of Brian who he thought might win the match,' said Chris.

Brian chose his words carefully, knowing that the conversation would be broadcast on both BBC Radio Nottingham and BBC Radio Derby. 'It's an impossible situation, John,' he said. 'I know everything in football – without being over-conceited, because you know I *am* a conceited man – but the only thing I've never seen is a football match where both sides win.'

Expertly sidestepping the direct question, Brian referred to the two managers. He said he knew Forest boss Paul Hart, having signed him from Leeds United, although he admitted he didn't know the Derby manager John Gregory. Nevertheless, he thought fondly of both clubs.

'I've got lovely thoughts about Forest and I have nothing but good thoughts about Derby,' said Brian. 'In this patch, we've brought the atmosphere of a derby match to the front of things. I've just come back from Newcastle and you know what it's like up there between Newcastle and Sunderland. The Middlesbrough stadium is absolutely magnificent. My brother-in-law is a Sunderland fanatic – I know when they've lost because he doesn't speak for a week!'

When Chris listened to my copy of this wonderful recording, it clearly brought back some special moments that could have been lost forever. The BBC hadn't kept a copy of the recording at the time, so he was grateful to hear it again all these years later.

'I still pinch myself when I think about it,' Chris told me. 'It felt like two old friends and colleagues having a chat. But typical Cloughie, he led the way and just jumped straight in from the start. Technically, John was the reporter, but at times Brian led the conversation. It was fascinating.'

The exchange between Brian and John about the fashion statements of players prompted Chris to think about how Cloughie would have handled players using social media these days.

'Can you imagine Brian Clough seeing his players posting on Twitter?' asked Chris on my *Green Jumper* podcast. 'Especially when you think about the things they write on Twitter these days and the arguments they get into. Let's be honest, if Twitter had been around in Cloughie's day, and he'd wanted to use it, he would have been brilliant. I suspect he would have had to be persuaded to use it, but he would have been superb. With all those one-liners, Twitter was made for Brian Clough.'

* * *

Another journalist who recorded a conversation between Clough and a footballing 'great' was Norman Giller. On that occasion, Old Big 'Ead was chatting to ex-England centre-forward Jimmy Greaves. When Greaves started working in the media, he launched a regular column in a national newspaper. 'Jimmy had just conquered a drinking problem, which was a miracle itself because he'd been lost to the bottle for five years,' said Giller, who became Greaves's biographer.

When Greaves started his newspaper column, the first phone call he received at home was from Cloughie, who insisted that his old England team-mate should get on the next train to Nottingham. Brian offered him an exclusive interview 'for nowt'. Giller recalled that it was quite a coup at the time because Brian was so in demand.

Jimmy and Norman did as they were told and travelled by train to Nottingham, with Norman taking a tape recorder with him. The two former colleagues were soon reminiscing as they sat in Cloughie's office at the City Ground.

'I would have paid to be the man taping on that day,' Norman told me on *Green Jumper*. 'I was a very lucky boy. It was wonderful listening to two old friends chewing over past times, both being very honest and frank with each other.'

When I suggested to Norman that it must have been difficult for him to admit to Clough and Greaves that he was running out of tape, he said that it had almost become a competition between the two of them to see who could get the first word in. 'Of course, Cloughie won that one!' added Norman.

When he returned to the newspaper office and began to transcribe the conversation, he had to cut out some of the more colourful language. But what do you expect from two of the most colourful figures in the history of English football? 'There was Brian, who'd just won two back-to-back European Cups, giving Jimmy this interview purely to give him a leg-up in his new career as a broadcaster,' Norman told me. 'It just showed the generosity of spirit of Cloughie.'

* * *

During the phone-in I wrote about earlier, Clough referred to Greaves as having been his idol. The comment came during a conversation with a caller towards the end of the programme, when Mark Shardlow said that Duncan was on the line to speak to Cloughie. If Duncan wasn't nervous before making the call, he probably was when he heard Brian's voice. 'Duncan, what do you want? And hurry up!'

'It's great to talk to you,' said Duncan, who immediately softened Clough's response by conveying his admiration. He wanted to know which matches Brian considered to be his greatest performances as a player – and as a manager too.

'As a player, I scored more goals than anybody else,' said Brian, who was probably referring to his goalscoring record of 251 league goals in 274 games.

'I used to work with Jimmy Greaves, who was my idol as a goalscorer. He was nippy, he was slim, he was beautiful, he played for the big clubs and he played for England. I don't see him now as regularly as I used to, but every time I saw him when I was working with him on television he used to say to me, "Don't tell me!" That's because I used to say to him, "Who scored the quickest 250 goals, Greavsie?" And he would say, "You did – but don't tell me every time you see me!" But I had to remind him. Scoring goals was my business. I could score goals, it's as simple as that.'

Knowing Greaves as well as he did, Norman Giller has no doubt that the former Spurs striker admired Clough's exploits in front of goal, 'Jimmy would bow the knee to Cloughie as a goalscorer. But he would also quietly point out that most of his were in the Second Division, whereas every one of Jimmy's 357 goals were in the First Division, which is a record that will never be beaten because that division has now gone.'

Greaves admitted that he regretted not taking the chance to play for Clough when he was manager of Derby. 'I heard that Brian Clough wanted to talk to me about a possible transfer but at the time I just wasn't interested,' he wrote in 1980. 'Looking back, I now realise that it would have been an excellent move for me. Brian may not have been able to stop my drinking, but I think he would have given me a few more years in the game.'

Instead of Derby, Greaves joined West Ham – a move he also regretted. 'I remember [Spurs manager] Bill Nicholson calling me into the office a couple of hours before the transfer deadline to tell me that he was signing Martin Peters and West Ham wanted me as part of the deal,' said Greaves. 'It seemed the logical move for me, but I know now that I shouldn't have gone. Bobby Moore and Geoff Hurst were getting on and they had a pretty poor side. How we stayed up that season I'll never know.'

* * *

The recording with Jimmy Greaves was not the first time that Norman had encountered Cloughie. The first time they met was in 1959, at England's training camp at Roehampton, 'The Brian Clough I met there was nothing like the Brian who later became a legend in his own lifetime. He was a quiet guy who wanted to take a back seat because he felt overawed by the likes of Bobby Charlton and Jimmy Greaves, two players he idolised.

'Brian was there with his Middlesbrough team-mate Edwin Holliday and they were both making their debut for England against Wales. Edwin was the character out of the two of them. He was the one you thought would make a good television personality. But of course it was Cloughie who came through as one of the forces of nature.'

Indeed, it was in front of a television camera that Cloughie recorded a golden moment at his home in Derbyshire, with Norman behind the scenes. They had a special visitor that day – the football commentator Brian Moore. The idea was to record a tribute to mark Moore's 30 years with ITV. On the evening before the recording, they were all sitting in Cloughie's lounge and having a conversation about their memories of working together when Clough decided to play one of his Frank Sinatra records. He began to recall stories of when he met Sinatra: it was the time Old Big 'Ead met Old Blue Eyes. The following day, memories of Sinatra hit the right note with Cloughie as he paid tribute to his favourite commentator.

Recalled Norman, 'We were filming in Cloughie's garden. Without Brian Moore knowing, I'd arranged for Brian Clough to make a presentation to the other Brian – a framed, autographed cartoon.' Then suddenly Cloughie appeared and began singing the George and Ira Gershwin song 'S'Wonderful'. 'It made great television,' said Norman. 'We got two minutes of Brian Clough serenading Brian Moore.'

Some years later, there was a poignant moment when Cloughie attended the funeral of Moore in a village church in Kent. Norman was giving the eulogy when he spotted Clough in the congregation. 'Hundreds of people were listening to the service outside,' Norman told me. 'I'm halfway through the eulogy when I look down and spot those "George Robey" eyebrows looking up at me. I managed to ad-lib about how thrilled Brian Moore would be that his dear friend Cloughie had made it to the funeral. He had been very ill so we didn't expect to see him. People actually applauded Cloughie in the middle of my eulogy.'

Norman told me he would always have fond memories of Clough, 'Not only as a great man of the beautiful game, but as a great human being, who did so much very quietly for charity and the people down on their luck. Brian was always the first to offer a helping hand in a quiet way. People thought he was bombastic, which he could be, but he did a lot of things quietly which didn't make the headlines. That was the real Brian Clough and the Brian Clough I want to remember.'

* * *

While writing this book, I found a copy of the video footage that Norman Giller referred to, in which Cloughie – quite literally – sings the praises of his friend Brian Moore. The admiration between the two men is palpable and you can sense a much softer side to Clough – not only because he no longer had the everyday pressures of football management to contend with, but because he was with a close friend too. The two men are shown sitting on a wooden bench in Cloughie's garden and chatting together for Moore's programme, *Over The Moon, Brian*. This is how that amazing footage played out:

BM, 'Life has moved on for you now. Tell me how you're coping.'

BC, 'You mean I've shot it?'

BM, 'No, you could never do that.'

BC, 'I'm loving every second. And people sometimes, Brian, don't believe me and they say, "How are you coping with retirement?" I'm loving it, man!'

As he says those final four words, Clough leans towards Moore, who is on his left, as if to emphasise that he means what he says.

BC continues, 'I should have done it five years ago.'

BM, 'Had it become that much more difficult over the years for managers to cope? I don't mean with tactical things, because you managed that, but with players' demands and so on. Had it become a much more difficult job?'

BC, 'Management has become harder in football regarding agents and players' demands and the absolute necessity that you have to succeed.'

BM, 'It's an easy thing to say, "It's not as good as it was." Is that something you subscribe to?'

BC, 'Well, I think it's as good as it was. Somebody gave me an OBE and the Queen asked me about football. And I said, "It's better than it's ever been."'

BM, 'Really?'

BC, 'Yes [pauses]. Now, as a friend, that's the first time I've told that to anybody.'
Brian Moore pauses, as this gem of information sinks in.

BM, 'I appreciate that. Did you get the impression that she was impressed by that?'

BC, smiling as he speaks, 'I think impressed is the wrong word, actually. I think she's interested in everything that goes about. I think she was looking forward to meeting me.'

BM, 'I'm sure.'

BC, wagging his finger to make the point, 'That's a *joke*!'

BM, 'Terrific [Brian Moore pats Cloughie on the arm]. Now, what's going to happen now?'

BC, 'Retirement-wise?'

BM, 'Yes.'

BC, 'Awe, I'm going to love it, man. You just get round to seeing me occasionally. I'm going to watch a bit of cricket. I might go to the West Indies, but I'll take your advice and not go for too long.'

BM, 'Do you think you might be tempted to come back into football?'

BC, 'Management-wise? Not a prayer. My son – my little son – who used to work with me, and now works with Liverpool, thinks that I should have taken a job at Forest or wherever – consultancy and all that type of thing. Not a prayer. Barbara and I have had enough of it. I don't mean that possibly as it sounds. The harshness of my voice doesn't mean that. We've done our stint. I'm 58 going on 98. I've done my stint, 41 years, and I'm looking forward to just watching the grass grow and smelling my roses and seeing a friend like you.'

Clough nods towards Moore as he says those last few words.

BM, 'Terrific. Well, I can only say that millions watching will say "thank you" for what you've given them, and I thank you for your friendship too.'

Clough appears overcome with emotion as he reaches out to shake Moore's hand, then holds it and kisses the back of his friend's hand.

An on-screen message appears, 'Over The Moon, Brian – The Sting.'

The footage switches to Clough, still in the garden, holding a large, framed present. As he walks towards the camera, he holds the frame in both hands.

BC, 'Brian thinks the programme's finished, but he knows nowt about television, actually. What he *does* know is that he's got thousands and thousands of friends. I feel like Michael Aspel[1] actually, giving him this. But he's survived in the game, which is a hard game, for so long it's incredible. And why he's survived is he's a charming man – and what's more important, he's good at his job.'

The film cuts to Brian Moore, still sitting on the wooden bench, speaking to the camera crew.

BM, 'Well, that's it, I think lads. That's a wrap.'

BC, 'Well unfortunately for you, Mr Moore, that wasn't a wrap. This is from ITV [Clough rests the framed present on the bench, facing Moore, and holds it steady]. Now, it's a present for a very special man – and a very special present.'

Moore starts to look at some of the many signatures surrounding a picture of him holding a commentary microphone. There are more than 60 signatures of famous sportspeople such as Sir Alf Ramsey and Sir Tom Finney.

BC, 'It's gorgeous.' Pointing to one of the signatures, he says, 'Tommy Lawton's your hero, which I find staggering because I scored more goals than him. Every single signature is on there.'

BM, 'Stanley Matthews.'

BC, 'Tom Finney. Everything. Now, we happen to think you're wonderful.'

Clough points towards his friend and starts singing.

BC, 'S'wonderful, marvellous, you should care for me.'

BM, 'And a flattering picture of me in the middle.'

BC continues singing, 'Awful nice, paradise, that's where you belong. You make my life so glamorous.'

At this point, the camera focuses on Moore's smiling face. He's a little unsure of what to make of Clough's impromptu musical tribute.

---

1   Michael Aspel hosted *This Is Your Life* in which he surprised celebrities by approaching them when they least expected it, and then took them straight to a TV studio for a special programme looking back on their life with family, friends and colleagues.

BC, 'You can't blame me for feeling amorous. S'wonderful, marvellous, that you should care for us.' Clough shakes Moore's hand.

BM, 'Terrific. Good song.'

BC, 'You're the only commentator that Barbara can listen to without getting irritated.'

BM, 'Well, I'm delighted to hear that. I'm absolutely choked up by that. What can I say? I'm over the moon, Brian.'

5

At Home With Cloughie

Very few journalists were invited into Brian Clough's home. He was well-known for being highly protective of his privacy and family.

While Chris Ellis was extremely fortunate, another of the lucky ones welcomed into the Cloughs' house in Derby was features writer Pat Parkin. It was the start of the 1967/68 season and the article in the *Derby Evening Telegraph* had the headline, 'At Home With The Cloughs'.

Pat described how Brian's public persona was nothing like the man she met in a domestic setting.

She wrote, 'The tough-talking bluff image of Derby County Football Club manager, Brian Clough, went up in smoke the moment he answered the door of his large detached home at Darley Abbey. With a baby in his arms, a boy at his feet, and toys everywhere, he looked just like any other harassed father.'

Brian's wife Barbara told Pat how her husband was very much a family man and that a 'hard exterior' covered up a very sensitive and sincere person. The couple had then been married for eight years and had already experienced the wonderful highs and terrible lows of football.

Those lows were described in detail, with Barbara referring to 'that black Christmas of 1962' when Brian suffered the awful injury which effectively ended his playing career. He had been playing for Sunderland on Boxing Day 1962 when Barbara, who was ill with flu, heard on her bedside radio the news that he had to be carried off the pitch on a stretcher.

The article went on to say that Barbara was naturally horrified to hear that Brian had been taken to hospital. Initially it was thought he had suffered a broken leg and she hoped that – if that was the case – it would eventually heal and he would still have the opportunity to play top-flight football again. But the injury was worse than feared and he played only two more league matches. Barbara said she was delighted when, shortly after his testimonial match at Sunderland, Brian became the league's youngest manager by becoming the boss of Hartlepools (they became Hartlepool in 1968).

Behind the scenes, Brian admitted that he didn't want football to take him away from seeing his family. Pat Parkin described him as being devoted to his three children: three-year-old Simon, 18-month-old Nigel and 12-week-old Elizabeth.

'No job is worth missing watching your kids grow up,' said Brian, 'and if the game does that for me then I shall have no hesitation in throwing it up.'

During Pat's visit, Barbara decided to go shopping in Derby. The article then quoted Brian speaking to his wife, 'Off you go love, I'll take care of the kids, and leave the washing up for me, too.'

Cloughie was clearly happy taking on the domestic honours – and of course football would present him with further opportunities to win domestic honours while Derby manager.

Continuing the subject of football – or 'soccer' as it was described – Brian said the only work commitment he had on the day of Pat's visit was watching a match in the evening. He'd be among a crowd of nearly 45,000 at the City Ground to watch Nottingham Forest draw 3-3 with Coventry in the First Division. One of the Forest scorers in that game was Ian Storey-Moore, whom Clough would later try to bring to Derby in 1972. In fact, Storey-Moore was paraded in front of the Rams fans as a new signing, only for the transfer to collapse at the last minute. Amid huge controversy, he was sold to Manchester United instead.

The next time Pat visited the Cloughs at home for another insightful feature in the *Derby Evening Telegraph* was in 1969, when Derby had won promotion to the First Division. Although the Rams had enjoyed success in the 1968/69 season, Barbara admitted that she had feared Brian might have been sacked the previous season.

'It's not that I didn't believe in him,' she said. 'I never had any doubts that Brian would be successful as a football manager – he could be a success at anything he put his mind to. But when the Rams ended last season in such a poor position, I was so depressed and disappointed for him.' Pat's article said that since that disappointing time, Barbara had been delighted with the more recent change in fortunes, 'I feel he has given success not only to the club but to the whole town, too.' The couple had enjoyed a quiet meal out on Easter Saturday as a joint celebration of their wedding anniversary and Derby County's promotion from the Second Division.

Towards the end of the article, it said that Barbara was finding it hard to adapt to life as the wife of a well-known personality. Pat quoted Barbara as saying that sometimes she gave a false name when making an appointment at the hairdressers so people didn't realise who she was, 'It's not that I'm not proud to be Mrs Brian Clough, but I don't know anything about football and I can't discuss it, so I've very little in common if people do come up and speak to me.'

However, when it came to predicting football results, Barbara was the one who completed the pools coupon – and asked Brian to post it, 'He tried to do one once, but he didn't know how to fill in the coupon, so now it's left to me to win the fortune.'

On Sundays, according to the article, Brian would ensure he spent time with his family. Sometimes that would involve playing football in the park, with the three children taking on the roles of Derby County players. Simon would be Roy McFarland and Nigel would become John Robson while Elizabeth (known as Libby) liked to be Kevin Hector.

This domestic scene showed the real Brian, said Barbara, 'When I read newspaper stories about the rough, tough Cloughie I never even associate the description with Brian – he just isn't that way at all. It's just an image he seems to have acquired.'

The tough exterior that Brian developed in his professional life was a million miles away from the family man described in the article, but it remained an invaluable suit of armour needed to tackle the harsh realities of football. Clough once said that his coach at Derby and Forest, Jimmy Gordon, was too nice to be a manager. Jimmy didn't have an enemy in the world, said Brian. 'As a coach, he's been a tremendous servant to me at Derby, Leeds and Forest,' he wrote in Gordon's testimonial programme in 1981, 'but I'm delighted for his sake that he never actually went into management.

'Jimmy is such a conventional sort of person that he liked to see the best in everybody and there have been times when he's said to me, "Leave him alone – he's a nice lad."

'It's all well and good but with that kind of attitude, Jimmy would have found himself relegated 93 times. Kenny Burns doesn't ask to be liked; John Robertson doesn't ask to be liked; Peter Shilton doesn't ask to be liked. It's what they do on the field of play that matters when you are running a successful football club.

'But there again, Jimmy Gordon doesn't ask to be liked – but I think he is, by everyone.'

* * *

Just like Pat Parkin had described the 'tough-talking' image going up 'in smoke' when he answered the door to her, in the years that followed Clough was keen to stress that he didn't rule by fear. Whether the players actually *liked* him was another matter completely. But he said that instead of criticising what players *couldn't* do, he gave encouragement by praising what they *could* do. In an interview I discovered from early 2004, he was asked about his methods of motivating players.

'I prided myself on getting a wee bit more out of them than *they* thought they had – and other people certainly didn't think they had,' he said. 'That was part of management … I took great pride in telling them how good they were. It wasn't a case of saying, "You can't do this and you can't do that." I used to say, "Blow me, when you played that ball, it was an absolute dream. When I was a player, I couldn't do that." And if they got a goal I used to say, "I used to put them in, but I didn't put them in as good as that." The fact I got five times more than them, they didn't even know.'

6

Walking on the Trent

When Cloughie appeared on a radio phone-in in November 2001, he reminded listeners of his ability to walk on water – and joked about the time he feared the big central defender Larry Lloyd was going to throw him into the River Trent.

The first caller to the programme on 106 Century FM said it was an honour to speak to 'a living legend'. During the hour-long chat, Clough answered questions about various topics including managerial sackings, player discipline and the fortunes of Forest and Derby. When asked how he was feeling, he replied, 'I'm in good nick. I'm on top of the world.'

One of the callers asked for his thoughts on the lack of discipline on the field. He said some managers found it a difficult issue. He said rules had to be enforced, by use of fines if necessary. Even if the player is 6ft 5in, 'I used to look up at Larry Lloyd and think that one of these days he's going to belt me and I'll finish up in the Trent. But I would have had no trouble in the Trent because I had a path I used to walk across.'

Brian was asked how he thought the likes of tough-tackling defenders Lloyd and Kenny Burns would have fared in the modern game, with red and yellow cards being dished out so freely.

'Oh, they'd have been all right, they'd have looked after themselves,' said Cloughie. Then came the punchline, "They wouldn't have got better looking, obviously." And their rugged appearance would have stood them in good stead, he said. 'They didn't have to tackle when we were working together,' he joked. 'They just had to look at the centre-forwards and that was enough.'

Although Brian liked to have a gentle jibe about Burns's appearance (he once said his dog was better-looking) he was also quick to praise the former Scotland international for the way he adapted to the role of sweeper, having previously been a centre-forward. During his years in retirement, Cloughie would speak with affection about 'Kenneth' and regarded him as a friend.

* * *

During one of his appearances on radio in 2003, Cloughie was asked whether he had ever considered returning to football in an advisory capacity, perhaps as a director of football at a club. The question prompted an answer which surprised me, even when listening back to the recording all these years later.

'I would have liked Forest, for example, having been there so long, to have asked [me] to have some little input to them over the last ten years I've been retired. First of all, I think I earned it. Secondly, I think I'm worth it. I think even at my age, with my enthusiasm and my knowledge, I could have contributed something to Nottingham Forest. And they never asked me.'

Brian added that if he had been approached by Forest, he wouldn't have overstepped the mark and interfered with the manager's job – something he was passionate about when he was in charge. 'I know the rules. Never encroach on the manager, never do that,' he said before illustrating the point by referring to Bill Shankly when he retired as Liverpool boss. 'Poor old Bill Shankly when he retired and I was in my prime, Bill used to go down to the training sessions and it was a bit of an awkward situation.' He said that he would never want to embarrass someone like the then Reds boss Paul Hart by infringing on his work – he would have a cup of tea and a chat with him instead. However, in classic Clough style, he added that he would have liked to have embarrassed Dave Bassett and David Platt when they were in the Forest hot-seat.

The programme host Darren Fletcher picked up on Brian's comments straightaway. He said it was the first time he had heard Brian say he would have liked to have been involved in Forest in some form after his retirement. 'I'm not surprised, because they say football is in your blood and never leaves you,' said Darren.

'I just don't want anyone to misinterpret what I'm saying,' added Cloughie. 'I'm not looking for a job. And with the fees you pay me, I'm certainly not looking for money. Now, if you believe that you believe anything!'

In other recordings I've collected, Brian spoke about some of the invitations he had received to get back into football. He said the former Southampton boss Lawrie McMenemy had asked whether he'd be interested in helping with the Northern Ireland team. Cloughie said he had also had a verbal approach from Leicester City when Martin O'Neill left for Celtic. But, as far as management roles were concerned, Brian was adamant he had retired and didn't want the day-to-day pressures that came with such a position. 'I get a tingle now and again when people appear to be making a mess of it,' he said. 'But I resist the temptation. I'm having such a good time.'

Indeed, there was certainly no harm in discussing a bit of 'Fantasy Football', if you can call it that. When he was asked which modern-day player he would have liked to have managed, there was no hesitation in the reply, 'I'd take the Frenchman from Arsenal.' For clarification, as the Gunners' French contingent was particularly strong at the time, Cloughie was referring to the legendary Thierry Henry, 'His pace, when he's running with the ball or challenging, is nothing short of incredible. His pace is the most deceiving thing in football. With the length of his legs, you don't think he's moving until he appears two yards past everybody … he glides and his ball control is second to none. His ability to hit the target on all occasions when he goes clear is nothing short of incredible.'

When Arsenal, including Henry, beat the record set by Clough's Forest of 42 league games unbeaten, the disappointment of seeing the achievement overtaken was softened by the sheer brilliance of that Gunners side. 'When I watch them I drool – and not because I'm nearly 70,' Brian told *The Sun*. 'It's because I see a team who have brought to football the art of simplicity. High technical skills, rhythm, a joy to behold. And the killer instinct.' He added that their disciplinary record had vastly improved and he praised manager Arsène Wenger. 'It is no exaggeration to say Wenger has become an idol of mine. And from somebody as conceited, biased, bigoted and big-headed as me, that is a compliment.'

In response, Wenger said, 'Clough says he idolises me. Maybe that is too much, but it is good to get such a compliment from him. I rate highly what he did at Nottingham Forest. It's incomparable. And the fact he likes the way we play football makes me so very proud.'

Wenger went on to say he hoped to match Cloughie's record of two European Cups (something he didn't manage to achieve, failing to win it even once at Arsenal). But he admitted that to achieve it with Forest's resources had been 'totally surreal in today's terms'.

During a visit to the City Ground in 2018, Wenger described Brian as 'a special person in English football'. He said the influence and quality of a manager had been much more important during Clough's era than it was in the modern game. 'Success has become much more predictable today than it was during that period,' said Wenger. 'It was only two foreign players, you had income shared equally because there was no television money and only the gates made the difference.' Plus, the art of scouting players and the opponents was more difficult in the past, he said. 'Today, all is available, it's easier. At the time you had to look. I spent time you would not believe to see how managers work, to travel with my car at night and watch the training in the morning and come back home again. It's different now – you go on the internet and you have every exercise of every single club. At the time, you had to fight for information. For me, Brian Clough was like a guy on another planet.'

It was fitting that – to help raise money for the Brian Clough statue in Nottingham – Wenger donated a shirt signed by Arsenal's unbeaten 2003/04 Premier League-winning 'Invincibles', which was auctioned off. The collectable redcurrant shirt had been designed for their final season at Highbury, in tribute to the shirts the players had worn in their first season at the ground in 1913. And in a perfect twist of fate, Forest historian Don Wright (my former editor at the *Newark Advertiser*) documents in his 2015 book *Forever Forest* how it was the Nottingham club who had originally donated a supply of their red shirts to the 'Royal Arsenal' for their first match in 1887.

But the last word on this whole subject of Arsenal, and the setting of a new unbeaten record, must go to Cloughie himself. 'The way they play is exceptional,' he said. 'They could have been nearly as good as us.'

7

Confession Time

As the title of this chapter suggests, it's time for a confession. It's something I've kept under wraps for more than 40 years. While sorting out some of the memorabilia I've collected, I came across an item which is the focus for this admission.

Bearing in mind that *FourFourTwo* magazine once described me as 'Cloughie's Number One Fan', and that I've conducted many media interviews over the years (as editor of the tribute website) trumpeting Clough's genius as a manager, I realise this confession will come as a surprise to some.

I'll cut to the chase. It goes back to a copy of *Shoot!* magazine from February 1981, when I publicly criticised Brian Clough for a decision he'd made to sell one of his players. I was so incensed by what had happened, just a few months after Clough's Nottingham Forest had been knocked out of the European Cup, that I wrote to *Shoot!* and explained how annoyed I was. This was obviously long before the days of emails or social media posts that are written in the heat of the moment. I wrote a letter setting out exactly why Clough had made a mistake.

Looking back, I jokingly blame it on being a young and naive football supporter who needed to let off steam. I was only 13 years old at the time, honest! Having supported Forest since 1977, when they were still in the old Second Division, I thought there was nothing unusual in your football team winning the championship title at the first attempt and then going on to win the European Cup twice in successive seasons. Surely Cloughie was losing the plot, after being knocked out of the European Cup and then selling one of his key players? My letter to *Shoot!* was dispatched (via the local post box) and I told no one else about it.

The editorial team at the magazine must have been impressed. My strongly worded views were included on the letters page of the edition published on 14

February 1981. Note the date! It was certainly not a Valentine's gift for Cloughie. But it turned out to be a red letter day for me – I was absolutely astounded to see my opinions in print on the 'Goal-lines' page of my favourite football magazine, alongside other letters sent from correspondents in Canada, Glasgow and Nigeria. There was my name at the bottom of the letter, 'Marcus Alton, Lowdham'.

And the focus of my Clough criticism? The sale of Reds stalwart Ian Bowyer to Sunderland. Alongside a photo of Bowyer in action for Forest, the letter was given a headline of 'Forest Boob'.

'Needless to say **I** wasn't the Forest Boob!' Bowyer was keen to explain, when I showed him the magazine more than 40 years later. Understandably, he had a huge smile on his face when he saw my letter for the first time, all these years later. 'That's fantastic, absolutely fantastic!' he said, leaning forward to get a closer look and realising that the name at the foot of the letter was the same as the person interviewing him for the *Green Jumper* podcast.

The letter itself began by saying that it was the management pair of Clough and Peter Taylor who, in my view, had made 'a very bad mistake' by selling Bowyer. It continued, 'If it hadn't been for Ian's experience and talented play over the last six and a half seasons then Forest wouldn't have had so much success as they have done.'

I went on to say that I would rather have seen striker Peter Ward leave the club, especially as Trevor Francis had returned from injury. I said that Bowyer's sale reminded me of Archie Gemmill's departure to Birmingham City a few months previously – a transfer I described as another 'bad mistake'. As was the case with Gemmill, fans would miss Bowyer's creative and experienced play, I said.

Although I was critical of the decision by the Forest management, in my defence I delivered a back-handed compliment in the final paragraph. I said that while I admired Clough and Taylor for what they had achieved at Forest in recent years, I also admired Ian Bowyer for the same thing.

The editor of the letters page added a comment underneath, in an attempt to balance the criticism. It read, 'Ian is 30 next birthday and the £250,000 Forest received represented good business.'

I would have loved to have shown the letter to Cloughie on one of the occasions I interviewed him during his retirement. But, honestly, I'd forgotten all about it. The magazine was in a box in the loft which was gathering dust. Without doubt, I'm sure that if I'd shown the *Shoot!* letters page to the Miracle Manager himself, he would have smiled and probably made a choice comment to put me in my place! Well, he had mellowed a little in retirement, after all. But I also think he would have been impressed that a 13-year-old fan felt strongly enough at the time to get his views into print. He would have also recognised that part of the letter was exactly spot-on.

'You may think that I'm making a mountain out of a molehill,' I wrote, 'but I don't think Bowyer will settle down and perform as well with Sunderland as he did at Forest.'

When I read that paragraph to Bowyer, he laughed out loud. History had proven that the would-be journalist from a village called Lowdham in Nottinghamshire was along the right lines. Within a year of joining Sunderland, Bowyer was back at the City Ground.

In my opinion, Bowyer was one of the unsung heroes of Forest's rise to international glory under Cloughie. In the 1979 *Nottingham Forest Annual*, Ian was described as 'Mr Versatility' because of the number of different positions he was able to play. 'It meant I could play a lot of different positions badly,' he told me modestly. It's that kind of self-deprecation that makes him even more impressive in my eyes. Don't forget, long before the European success at Forest, he had won the League Cup and European Cup Winners' Cup as a teenager at Manchester City.

Bowyer's versatility was clear for all to see during an eight-day period in March 1978. A Saturday match against West Bromwich Albion in the FA Cup saw him deputise for Viv Anderson at right-back. On the following Tuesday he played centre-forward against Leicester City because Peter Withe was suspended and the following Saturday he was in midfield to face Liverpool – in the League Cup Final at Wembley.

Looking back, Bowyer told me that the only position he hadn't played during his career was centre-half. But with the likes of Larry Lloyd and Kenny Burns taking care of that part of the defence, his agility and naturally powerful engine to get him effortlessly around the pitch meant his physique and skill was better suited elsewhere.

However, he did admit to going in goal, not once but twice. On the first occasion he put on the goalie's gloves after Forest keeper John Middleton was injured during a match at Oxford in 1975. Bowyer was between the sticks for the second half of the game and the Reds won 1-0. 'With an emphasis on the *nil*,' added Bowyer, who is still proud to have kept a clean sheet that day.

The second time he was called upon to keep goal was during his second stint at Forest. Bowyer recalled that Steve Sutton was injured during a match against Leicester City and once again he did the honours as the last line of defence. He even saved a penalty from Leicester's Gary McAllister. But the referee ordered the spot-kick to be retaken because Bowyer was adjudged to have moved before the talented Scot had kicked the ball. Although the stand-in keeper blocked the second attempt, the ball rebounded to McAllister. 'He put the ball, me and everything else into the net,' says Ian. And who can blame him for perhaps still feeling a little sore after such a sterling effort in the number one jersey?

During Forest's first season back in the top flight in August 1977, and with John Middleton in goal, Bowyer had been selected by Cloughie as part of the team which beat Everton 3-1 in the opening fixture at Goodison Park. But it was not all plain sailing. A newspaper cutting I discovered in 2022 from Liverpool's *Football Echo* that season included a story, told by Bowyer, that I had never heard before. After further league victories in August against Bristol City and Derby County, Clough's Forest (including Bowyer wearing number eight) crumbled to a 3-0 defeat at Arsenal on 3 September. That result turned out to be a defining one for the rest of the season, after the critics predicted it was all over for the newly promoted side. 'They said that was the end, but really it was the beginning,' said Bowyer.

He told the *Echo*, 'Not much was said after the match, but then on Monday we gathered in one of the guest rooms at the ground where we normally have our team talks. For well over half an hour the verbal battle raged, it was a real ding-dong. Each individual was analysed as well as the team.

'It wasn't all one way, we were given a chance to put our point of view, but the message from the boss was that we had not done ourselves justice and that we had not competed as we should.'

Bowyer concluded that this meeting had helped the team for the rest of the season. 'Things really started to hum from then and there is no doubt that Arsenal did us a real favour in administering that heaviest defeat of the season,' he said.

Bowyer was one of the scorers in the next game, a 3-2 win at Wolves – among seven victories and two draws in the following nine matches after the Arsenal defeat.

* * *

All these years later, and with my *Shoot!* letter pulled from the archives, I was keen to know the story behind Bowyer's move from Forest to Sunderland – and why he was back at the City Ground just 12 months later. Ian told me that the transfer to the north-east suited all parties at the time. He was one of the few players the Reds could receive a transfer fee for and they needed the cash. Bowyer's former Forest team-mate Frank Clark was the assistant manager at Sunderland and that connection was key to the move.

'At the time, we'd been knocked out of the European Cup by the Bulgarian side Sofia, and so the club had a rethink,' said Bowyer. 'Many of us in the team were getting older together and in no time at all we lost the likes of Larry Lloyd and John McGovern. So, I was one of the players that they could get a fee for.'

Clark and the Sunderland boss Ken Knighton had travelled to Forest's team hotel before a match against Bolton to discuss the details of Bowyer's transfer. The discussion is documented in a column written by the Reds' then secretary Ken Smales in 1981. He described how good it was to meet up with Clark, the former Forest defender, once again.

'Little did I realise that he and Ken were at Bolton on business,' wrote Smales, 'although I should really have guessed, because they would not waste time travelling down from the north-east to watch a match for watching's sake.'

The managerial pair from Sunderland joined Clough, Taylor and Smales for lunch and the transfer deal was eventually agreed, even though Smales admitted 'the penny didn't drop with me' about what was happening until sometime later.

I'm also pleased to read that Ken Smales shared the same kind of sentiment towards Bowyer that I had aired in my *Shoot!* letter. He wrote, 'He [Bowyer] is of the very fabric from which the success of this club has been woven these past few years and we all wish him well in the future.'

Bowyer had been signed from Orient by Dave Mackay in October 1973 for a bargain price of £40,000. But within a couple of weeks of the signing, Mackay had left Forest to become manager at Derby County – where the now-departed Clough had earlier used the Scot's experience to turn him into the linchpin of the Rams' success. Mackay's move from Spurs ensured his playing career was not only extended but richly rewarded with further honours. Similarly, some observers thought Bowyer's move from Forest to Sunderland might draw comparisons with Mackay's role as the veteran leader at Derby. But Bowyer was keen to dispel any thoughts of that kind. 'I'm not a Dave Mackay type of player, likely to make a dramatic impact,' he said at the time. 'My way is quieter – I'm used to an ordered, disciplined sort of football.'

The week after my letter was published, *Shoot!* dedicated a whole page to Bowyer's transfer. In it, Bowyer commented, 'In my first few days at Roker there was plenty of talk in the north-east about the amount of experience I've got. That's all right as long as the fans don't make me out to be grandad.

'A lot of people seem to think that my situation is similar to that of Dave Mackay when he left Tottenham for Derby. But that's not true – Mackay was nearly at the end of his career. I'm not.'

Bowyer went on to say that he felt he had four or five years of his playing career left. He said he was not moving to Sunderland as a quick stop on the way to retirement. Both he and Ken Knighton were confident that the young players at Roker Park would also benefit from his experience. 'Bowyer's very presence puts almost half the team under pressure,' said Knighton. 'And that's the way I like it. About five players will be wondering if Ian is going to get their shirt.'

Frank Clark was quoted as saying that Ian had often been underrated by the fans, but not in the dressing room. 'He has always been a players' player,' said Clark. But the biggest praise came from Brian Clough himself, 'Ian Bowyer has been the best professional at Forest, and I told him so earlier this season in front of all the players. While he was with us, he never caused us one second of trouble.' Clough said that his former club needed Bowyer's help as they fought to steer clear of the First Division relegation zone. 'I'm sorry to see him go,' added Clough, 'but it was a transfer that suited everybody.'

However, as I had predicted in my letter, Bowyer wasn't able to settle down at Sunderland. After just a few appearances he suffered the most serious injury of his entire career, a medial ligament problem in his right knee. During his spell in hospital, Knighton and Clark departed Roker Park and – once he was fit again – Bowyer decided he wanted to leave too. He was unimpressed by Sunderland's new manager, the former Derby County star, Alan Durban. Clough was only too delighted to welcome Bowyer back to Forest. Not only because he knew he could rely on Bowyer's experience and versatility – but because Forest could sign him for a fraction of the £250,000 they had sold him for.

Bowyer enjoyed a wonderful second spell at the City Ground, helping Forest finish fifth in the First Division in 1982/83, by which time Cloughie was now flying solo after Peter Taylor had decided to come out of a short retirement and rejoin Derby County. Towards the end of that season, Bowyer scored four goals in a run of seven wins and two draws which saw Forest storm up the table to secure a return to European football. He told the media at the time that he was glad to be back. 'There is an aura of success around Brian Clough,' he said. 'He has worked a miracle at Forest and those around him feel he will continue to do so.' Reflecting on the absence of Taylor, Bowyer said, 'The people who asked if the bubble had burst just didn't know Brian Clough.'

For five seasons in his second spell at Forest, Bowyer was a regular in the first team, helping the club finish in the top half of the table each time – with a third-place finish in 1984. Despite the highly controversial UEFA Cup semi-final against Anderlecht documented elsewhere in this book, Bowyer enjoyed playing alongside the new generation of Forest stars. 'For me, there was the satisfaction to watch so many young players come through,' he told me. He then named a few of them: Stuart Pearce, Des Walker, Chris Fairclough, Steve Hodge, Peter Davenport and of course Nigel Clough, to mention just a selection. The young Reds, who would go on to win silverware in their own right, clearly benefitted from Bowyer's experience.

No wonder, then, that Cloughie was pictured giving Bowyer a kiss on the cheek when the time came for his testimonial. Firstly, a grandly titled 'Testimonial Banquet' was held at the Royal Hotel on Wollaton Street in Nottingham in February 1986. I've got a copy of the four-page programme for the evening, incorporating the menu which included grilled rainbow trout, roast leg of lamb and a meringue nest filled with black cherries and cream. Sounds tasty! The schedule for the evening stated the meal would be served at 8pm, with a toast by 'Mr B.H. Clough' and the star cabaret was singer Vince Hill. No doubt his musical repertoire included his 1960's hit 'Edelweiss' from the musical *The Sound of Music*. Fifteen months later, there was the sound of applause at the City Ground as Bowyer waved goodbye at his testimonial against Derby. 'The Trent End were marvellous,' he told the *Nottingham Evening Post* after the match. And rightly so. Bowyer had given his all. In the week running up to the game, he had insisted on receiving twice-daily treatment on his dodgy ankle – 'so that I don't let anybody down'.

At the time of his transfer to Sunderland in 1981, thoughts of such a testimonial match had been a million miles away. He told the media at the time, 'At first, I had mixed feelings about the deal, especially as there would have been a testimonial for me before too long. But I reckoned by then I could just be a reserve – and who wants to know when you are not in the first team?' It's a credit to Bowyer that he maintained a first-team place when he returned to Forest. When I suggested to him that it appeared he always got on well with Cloughie, he didn't disagree – although he admitted they got off to a shaky start.

Back in the summer of 1975, just a few months after Clough's arrival, Bowyer was out of contract at Forest. He told the Professional Footballers' Association about the offer the club had made to him and the PFA said he had every right to a free transfer and could just walk away. 'At this time, I was playing up front during a pre-season tour of Northern Ireland and we scored six goals,' recalled Bowyer. 'I scored five and the other was an own goal.' Understandably, despite being in dispute with the club, Bowyer felt he was in a strong position. Forest appealed against the free transfer and a hearing was arranged at the Football Association headquarters in London. Club secretary Ken Smales accompanied Bowyer on the train to the capital while Clough travelled separately.

'I remember Brian didn't particularly want to go into this meeting,' Bowyer told me. The manager's choice of clothing probably reflected how he felt about the occasion. He walked into the offices at Lancaster Gate wearing his green sweatshirt and shorts. In other words, Cloughie wanted to show the FA that he had better things to do than spend his time at a hearing involving a player transfer. Bowyer recalled how, when it was over, they all walked out of the Lancaster Gate door and – because of Clough's matchday attire – a taxi driver shouted towards him, 'Cloughie, have you lost your dugout?'

'So, I don't think he particularly enjoyed the day,' said Ian. 'But we managed to agree something and I'm absolutely delighted to say that the best thing I ever did was to stay.'

Two European Cup medals, along with other honours, are evidence enough for that conclusion. After Bowyer's crucial match-winning header away at Cologne in the European Cup semi-final second leg in 1979, Clough declared that Bowyer was worth £1m. 'Mr Versaliity' had also scored in the first-leg 3-3 battle at the City Ground, after which some observers had said the odds were too heavily stacked against Forest reaching the final. At the post-match press conference in Cologne, Clough described the game as 'unbelievable'. When asked whether 'million-pound man' Trevor Francis would play in the final, the manager replied, 'He is in the squad.' He was then asked to comment on Bowyer's performance and stated, 'I think Ian Bowyer is worth a million.'

When I asked Bowyer about that comment, a smile flashed across his face, 'He [Clough] said to me after the match, "That goal is worth millions of pounds to the club and that will be reflected in the next pay rise you come in for." Well, I'm still waiting for that pay rise …'

Nevertheless, his admiration for Cloughie is as strong as ever. Would he still play for Clough if he had his time again, I asked. 'I always say that, with Brian, 99 per cent would play for him again. And I'm not the exception.'

8

An Audience With ...

The label on the cassette reads 'Football Forum'. Listening back to the recording, it should read 'An Audience With Brian Clough'.

It was October 2002 and Cloughie was part of a three-man panel answering questions from the audience. Sitting to his left was Dave Mackay, a legendary player and manager with Derby County and a former boss at Nottingham Forest. Even Mackay admitted during this event that it was really 'The Brian Clough Show'. The former Reds striker Garry Birtles was also on the panel but – quite understandably – he sometimes found it difficult to get a word in.

Brian Clough had the audience in the palm of his hand throughout the event held at Derby County's Pride Park Stadium. All these years later, it was still as entertaining and fascinating to listen to as when the recording was originally made. In fact, towards the end of the forum, Clough delivered the type of wonderful one-liner that could rival his most famous quote. I'll have to add it to the list of classic quotes on the tribute website.

After launching brianclough.com in August 2000, I set up an online poll to decide Cloughie's all-time top quote. The winner was the comment I'd discovered in a regional television interview. The quote had gone unnoticed at the time, but I lifted it from the archives and included it in the list of golden comments Clough had spoken or written over the years.

'I wouldn't say I was the best manager in the business, but I was in the top one.' You just can't beat that for a Clough quote. You can even imagine the slight smile that appeared on his face a few seconds after finishing the sentence and letting it sink in, as the interviewer tried to continue the conversation without chuckling.

If you listen carefully to another brilliant quote from a 1972 television interview, you can hear the reporter trying to stifle a laugh after the delivery of another gem.

Clough is asked, 'What do you do when a player disagrees with you?' The answer is perfect, 'We talk about it for 20 minutes and decide I was right.'

Both of those wonderful quotes are etched on the paving around the Brian Clough statue in Nottingham. Now, for the first time, this book can add another to the classic quote collection. But I'll come back to that in a little while. Thanks to the recording of the forum, there are plenty more brilliant Clough comments to talk about first.

As the football discussion gathered pace, expertly chaired by the sports presenter Darren Fletcher, the conversation turned to an issue which is still a hot topic these days: video technology to assist referees. Brian was unsure that it would be a good move to introduce video replays to help the officials make decisions during a match.

'I feel there are enough interruptions as it is,' said Cloughie. He explained that the on-field 'action' during a match already lasted only 80 of the allotted 90 minutes, when various stoppages were taken into account. Allowing the play to be delayed further, to allow 'an extra linesman' to look at a replay and make a decision, would simply delay things even more. That, in turn, would bore the crowd and could even send some to sleep, he said.

Clough went on to say that it was 'part and parcel of the game' to have valid goals disallowed, or to be judged as being offside when a player is actually onside. He was adamant that too many stoppages in a match could kill the instant excitement and enjoyment that both supporters and players had come to expect.

'We don't want to destroy what we like to see in a football match,' said Brian. Thinking about a situation where a match would have two referees in charge – one on the field and one in a studio somewhere – Clough commented, 'If you're not careful, the equivalent is having two chairmen per club. Hey, one is enough!'

Garry Birtles, on the other hand, was in favour of the idea of video technology assisting the officials. He explained that some players were so fast ('flying machines like Thierry Henry') that referees couldn't keep up with the play. His comments in support of what we now call a Video Assistant Referee (VAR) are still part of the debate today.

'I think certain decisions cost football clubs a hell of a lot of money, it could cost them trophies,' said Birtles. 'I don't think it takes any time at all for a guy sitting in a studio somewhere to say to a referee with an earpiece either, "No, you were wrong" or, "Yes, you were right," and then just get on with it like that. Every other sport but football seems to be embracing it.'

Dave Mackay's thoughts went back to the 1966 World Cup Final and Geoff Hurst's controversial extra-time goal that gave England a crucial 3-2 lead against

West Germany. The ball hit the crossbar and bounced, with the linesman indicating it had crossed the line. In 2016, Sky Sports used their video technology to show it was the correct decision and that the ball had, indeed, gone over the line. Hurst's subsequent hat-trick, to make it 4-2, put the result beyond doubt, but Mackay was still keen to explain why he thought video technology was a good thing.

'I was at Wembley when England won the World Cup,' he said. 'Watching the game, I didn't think the ball *had* gone over the line. But seeing it on television in slow motion, it *did* go over the line. If the referee had not given the goal, England may not have won the World Cup and you can't get more serious than that.' Mackay concluded that video technology should be used for serious issues during a game.

When asked what he thought about the standard of refereeing at the time, Mackay's assessment was that 'the game has gone a little bit soft'. He said he didn't like to see yellow cards handed out for 'every little challenge'. But he said referees should be stronger when dealing with players who swear at them. 'Send them off,' he said, and it would soon put a stop to players who go around 'effing and blinding' at the officials. I think that's still food for thought these days when you lip-read some of the on-field abuse.

* * *

Part of the forum also focused on one of Cloughie's legendary television appearances: that remarkable head-to-head discussion with the former Leeds United boss Don Revie, just hours after Brian had been sacked as manager at Elland Road. He'd lasted for just 44 days in the role. A member of the audience at the forum questioned Clough about that infamous exchange between the two men, 'It looked like you didn't get on well with Don Revie – how well did you get on with him?' It was a question that Brian took head on. 'It was difficult to build bridges straightaway because he taught the art of cheating in football,' came the reply. 'That particular Leeds side were an absolute disgrace and there was no need for them to do it because they were good without it.'

Clough went on to describe how he disliked the Leeds players gathering around the referee when a decision went against them. He said it was intimidating and that, back then, referees 'were shaking before they went to referee a Leeds match'. He recalled watching a Leeds player who had perfected the art of time-wasting by bending down to pick up the ball but then 'accidentally' kicked it away as he attempted to pick it up, 'The ball would roll 15 yards and he'd walk after it, or he'd jog on the spot as if he was running.'

The archive footage of that conversation between Clough and Revie demonstrates that there was no love lost between the two men. Clough told the forum that when he went on the television programme he didn't want to hide how he felt – 'and I didn't hide it from Don Revie,' he added. But he said he *did* admire Revie for how he had picked Leeds up by the bootstraps and transformed them.

'Leeds was like a tip when he first went there,' said Clough. He likened United's transformation to the way Bill Shankly had breathed new life into Liverpool in the early 1960s. 'So you've got to give him [Revie] credit for that. I just felt that they were doing things they shouldn't have done and were getting away with it. I just wanted them exposing. Simple as that.'

* * *

When it comes to admitting mistakes, it's fair to say that Cloughie wasn't usually at the front of the queue. The 'we talk about it for 20 minutes' quote is evidence enough. So it was fascinating to hear his response at the forum when he was asked about poor signings he'd made. More specifically, the question from the audience was, 'Who were your worst signings at Derby and Forest?' The answer produced a superb Clough one-liner to add to the classics.

Brian's answer began by putting his many decisions into perspective, 'I've been in management many years and I've dropped some clangers, haven't I? Hey, I don't remember too many, because the good ones outweigh the bad ones.' He explained that if you worked in football management for a considerable amount of time, as he had done, it was inevitable that you would make mistakes – or 'drop clangers' as he liked to describe them.

'You pick the wrong side sometimes. You sign the wrong players or you say the wrong word. It's part and parcel of the job.'

Then came the punchline, 'Nobody's perfect. The nearest that you can see perfection – I'm right here.' The laughter from the audience turned into rapturous applause.

At the end of the evening, Cloughie burst into song, giving a short rendition of 'You've either got or you haven't got style'. He then remarked, 'And we've got it, haven't we?' The applause which followed showed that his fans had enjoyed every moment.

9

First Impressions

Long before the days of *Spitting Image* and its foam puppets of famous people, the world of impersonations was a much simpler place. Light-entertainment TV programmes featured impressionists who were actually human. Stars like Mike Yarwood and Janet Brown were regulars on Saturday night television. Politicians were usually the ones being impersonated: Yarwood would take-off the likes of Edward Heath and Harold Wilson while Brown was well-known for her version of Margaret Thatcher – she even made a record entitled 'The Iron Lady' and performed it on *Top of the Pops*.

It was only a matter of time before Brian Clough's headline-grabbing comments and charisma made him another character to add to Yarwood's repertoire. His various mannerisms and strong nasal drawl during TV interviews were a natural focus for a visual performer like Yarwood.

In a BBC interview I found from August 1975, Clough was asked what he thought about Yarwood's impression of him. He laughed before giving his answer, 'I think it's a great compliment he pays me for a start. I know him reasonably well from meeting him. He worries about his profession.' Brian was astounded that Yarwood himself had asked him whether he thought his impersonation was a good one. 'How the hell do I know that?' he said. 'All I know is that my kids fall off the settee watching him. For the first few times I never saw him – I wasn't in to see it. And then when he did me on certain things I thought, my God, this can't be right, it's *too* good. But I don't mind it at all. I've watched him on stage and on television and every time I watch him, people around me laugh.'

The former Derby and Forest winger Alan Hinton told me how he had originally met Yarwood in a club where the performer was starring in a cabaret show, 'I watched him at the Talk of the Midlands and I saw him in the bar afterwards and he asked me, "Do you think Mr Clough would object if I took him off and impersonated him?" I said, "Michael, he will love it." And of course, he did.'

It was Clough's self-assured performances as a TV pundit during the 1970 World Cup in Mexico that first caught the eye of the young impressionist. Speaking before his 'take-off' of Brian in Lulu's Saturday night TV show in July 1970, Yarwood said he'd admired Clough's performance on television, 'I know a lot of people thought he was a bit of a know-it-all, but that was what he was there for. He certainly made a big impact on me and I only include people who produce that sort of effect.'

Yarwood said he had carefully studied Clough's commentaries during the World Cup and had cancelled all engagements for the duration of the competition so he could watch at home. 'I can't say that Brian was very difficult to capture,' he admitted. 'He's got that distinctive north-eastern drawl which is a help. I don't anticipate that Brian will be annoyed in any way with my impression of him. Certainly, Mr Heath and Mr Wilson weren't … I think they were quite flattered, really … I hope Brian takes it the same way. I think he's a great personality. He'd make a very good theatrical agent!'

Yarwood was reported to have helped TV producer Rod Taylor with his portrayal of Clough in a theatre production later that year. Wearing a swept-back wig, Taylor (yes, I know – the 'alternative' Clough and Taylor!) gave an impersonation of Brian during the show *Up The Rams* at Derby Playhouse. The production was described in the *Derby Evening Telegraph* as a 'bawdy documentary on the history of Derby County'. Taylor, who usually worked behind the scenes in TV light entertainment, had been 'coached' for the part by Yarwood, for whom he had written the Clough sketch for the Lulu show earlier in the year. They'd come up with the idea of the impersonation during a dinner party. However, in a self-deprecating manner, Taylor described his stage debut as 'a poor man's version of Mike Yarwood doing an impersonation of Brian Clough'. It was certainly a brave venture in a place where the manager of the local football club was both a national celebrity and a respected manager. The big question was: would local fans really want to see the boss of their club being 'sent up' in this way?

The *Derby Evening Telegraph*'s review of the production was not exactly glowing. The reviewer, named as 'GDH', wrote, 'I didn't like it and I think most of the audience at last night's opening did not like it either. We went not knowing what to expect and most of us came away not a great deal wiser.' GDH said the production was not 'theatre' in any of the accepted senses, 'It comes nearest to being pantomime with the character of Brian Clough the fairy godmother, demon king, dame and Prince Charming all rolled into one.' Rod Taylor was described as giving 'a quite remarkable performance. It's a caricature as blatant as could be but it's alive – the only living character among a horde of cardboard cut-outs as impersonal as the figures in the stands that make up the set.' Ouch!

The reviewer concluded that, with the right audience, the show could be 'a riot'. But apparently a similar venture – a musical about Bolton Wanderers – had failed in Bolton because people interested in the theatre did not want a show about football, while those interested in football did not want to go to the theatre. That creative conundrum will always be a challenge. But one production where it succeeded beyond all expectations was at Nottingham Playhouse, where the tribute play, *Old Big 'Ead, In The Spirit of the Man*, was highly acclaimed. Football fans, many of whom had never set foot inside a theatre before, filled the place night after night.

The inspired choice to play Clough in this popular play was the actor Colin Tarrant, well known for his role as Inspector Andrew Monroe in the TV police drama, *The Bill*. Not only was Colin a Clough fan, he was also a superb impersonator of the Miracle Manager. I was invited to meet Colin by the playwright Stephen Lowe several weeks before the production began in 2005. We chatted about our memories of Cloughie and Colin became a very good friend. There was no hesitation when he agreed to my request to help launch the fundraising appeal for the Clough statue in Nottingham a few months later. And my fiancée Sarah and I were delighted when he accepted the invitation to attend our Clough-themed wedding in 2007. Not only that, but during the ceremony, in the grand ballroom of Nottingham Council House (the scene of many trophy celebrations), Colin recited a special poem I'd written, Clough style. At the wedding reception, held at the now-closed Ilkeston restaurant, Cloughie's, Colin sat on the same table as members of Brian's family. It was a truly memorable occasion and we will always think fondly of Colin. Sadly, he passed away in 2012, but the memories of his friendship and superb portrayal of Cloughie in the tribute play will stay with me forever.

Colin captured Cloughie's character and charisma brilliantly, from the moment he walked on to the stage in that famous green top and tracksuit bottoms. And the portrayal of Brian wasn't simply about repeating the words 'young man' in that distinctive northern drawl – it was much more than that. Colin had clearly studied his subject with painstaking accuracy. Even down to the way he used to scratch his head.

Old Big 'Ead in The Spirit of the Man was not a biography as such, although it did include biographical parts. One poignant moment saw him step back into the 1950s when he first met Barbara. In another touching scene he reflected on his relationship with Peter Taylor and regretted not making it up with his old pal after they fell out.

The play, enthusiastically supported by Clough's family, had been carefully constructed by Lowe and director Alan Dossor, backed by a talented cast. It worked on several levels and wasn't purely about football. There were some great one-liners too. When a struggling playwright called Jimmy became exasperated with the presence of Cloughie's spirit, he told him, 'You're not meant to be here, you don't exist!'

The reply was instant, 'You don't expect a little thing like that to bother Brian Clough, do you?' In that moment, the audience's applause was also instant. The critical acclaim included a wonderful review in *The Times*. I've still got the newspaper cutting – here's an excerpt of Jeremy Kingston's assessment,

> 'Whenever Colin Tarrant's Clough is dishing out the advice, with football his guide at all times, the fun is tremendous. Tarrant has turned himself into an astonishingly lifelike resemblance of the original. The widow's peak and dense eyebrows are easy to recreate, as is that odd habit of wobbling his head around as though uncertain of his neck. But Tarrant also catches the nasal voice, almost a whine, the often expressionless face and the rapid delivery of the lines Lowe gives him … it is Tarrant's Clough who makes the show worthwhile. Which is only what the original would have foretold.'

The Observer described how 'the blunt, inspirational manager Brian Clough is brought vividly back to life'. The reviewer, Susannah Clapp, wrote, 'It doesn't recreate episodes on the pitch or in the stands. It's entirely Clough-driven, as its subject would have wished.'

The sports pages of *The Times* also devoted two columns to 'Old Big 'Ead'. Nottingham journalist David McVay (Cloughie would have approved of 'David' rather than 'Dave') was given a byline for his review which described it as 'an overwhelming success for the man in the green tracksuit'. McVay also spoke to Stephen Lowe who produced a brilliant quote when explaining that he didn't want to upset any Clough supporters, of which there would be many in Nottingham. Lowe said, 'It is a bit like playing the Pope in the Vatican. You have to be careful.' In the same way that Tarrant sang an adapted version of Sinatra's 'My Way', Lowe managed to hit exactly the right note. A report in the *Nottingham Evening Post* began, 'Not for the first time this year, the Forest faithful were in tears. Last month it was relegation to the third tier of English football. Last night it was the premiere at the Playhouse of the drama inspired by Brian

Clough, under whom the Reds were champions of Europe.' One fan, wearing a Forest away shirt for his visit to the theatre, declared, 'Fantastic. I was crying at the end.' A Notts County supporter in the audience commented, 'It's one for the neutrals. You don't need to be a football fan to enjoy it.' The *Post*'s reviewer, Jeremy Lewis, wrote, 'This lovely play is not simply a celebration of the incomparable Brian Clough. It is a celebration of his greatest quality – the inspirational leadership that helped others to rise above themselves.'

The success of the production in attracting many newcomers to the theatre resulted in a national tour in 2006. I remember interviewing Colin for my tribute website before the tour began and asked him whether he felt the play would travel well. 'I'm sure it will,' he said. 'Brian Clough was one of those people who belongs to the national family, like Ronnie Barker. Brian has a special place in people's affections with the joy he brought to so many people.'

Born in Shirebrook and a Nottingham Forest fan, Colin felt honoured to have the role. 'I'm aware I'm dealing with a genuine national and international hero,' he told me. 'He was a great man in every way, a fantastic character. And, as such, a terrific subject for drama.' Colin revealed that he first learned about the play after reading about it in his dad's local newspaper. After years of privately imitating Cloughie for family and friends, he felt the role was perfect for him and contacted his agent straightaway. 'I'm told I can do a pretty accurate imitation. It's funny, but the minute you start to imitate Brian Clough, people start to laugh. You're not trying to laugh at him, it's just the mannerisms and vocal quirks. I've always latched on to them – not for the way he said things, but what he said. He was like a walking quote machine. I don't mean to sound flippant, he just had a wonderful wit about him.'

I was also fortunate to interview Stephen Lowe and Alan Dossor before the curtain went up for the first time. Stephen, who had written for such a national institution as *Coronation Street*, said he was very conscious of writing about a man who had also been a national treasure. 'It's like you're writing about everyone's family,' he told me. 'You have to be very careful and very sure you've captured the heart of the man – or as we call it, the spirit of the man.' Stephen and Alan had turned down a television project about Cloughie some years before the play took shape. They felt it wasn't right. But after the public's outpouring of grief following Brian's death in 2004, Stephen was approached again, this time for the theatre. 'It was that sheer overwhelming feeling,' said Stephen. 'And it was just so moving to see how people reacted to his life. He held a very special quality in our hearts and I really was moved by all that. I wanted to have something where we can say, "Thanks Brian, you're fun."'

Alan was an experienced TV and theatre director, having worked with many big names in the world of acting, such as Julie Walters, Alison Steadman and Pete Postlethwaite. I discovered that Stephen and Alan had decided not to pursue the previous idea of a television project because of the involvement of people that Alan characteristically described as 'blokes in suits'. Indeed, Alan, who passed away in 2016, described these people in similar tones to Cloughie talking about some football directors! He explained, 'Usually, when you're commissioned and invited to do something, mainly for television, a load of blokes in suits say, "We've got a fantastic idea." They then proceed to tell you exactly what it should be like and how they want it done. The only thing they can't do is either write it, or do it. In other words, they are exactly the same as what Brian Clough thought of football directors. They know **** all! You then have to try to create something that will satisfy them. And in the end, you find it hardly involves you at all. You're just doing what they want.'

This play, however, was completely different. I could tell it was a labour of love for both writer and director. 'I started watching Forest in the 1960s and I came back to Nottingham in 1984 and spent many years watching Cloughie work,' added Alan. 'My only regret is that he can't come and watch me work. But I'm sure he'll be watching from the clouds and I fully expect to hear a clap of thunder on the first night and a voice saying, "You've got that bit wrong, young man!"'

At the end of the play's national tour, which included visits to Brighton, Billingham, Birmingham and Sunderland, the production returned to Nottingham for a gala performance, attended by members of Brian's family and his former players. 'I know I'll be nervous again,' Colin told me ahead of that special night. 'It's live theatre and I am sure the butterflies will be kicking in again.' He said he had been delighted to have taken the play on tour after the success of the initial run. 'I was completely overwhelmed by the response of the audiences [in Nottingham],' he said. 'It was tremendous to have consistent standing ovations from a home crowd. And it was fantastic to have family and friends come to see the play and to meet up with them afterwards on those lovely summer nights. Very often I didn't know they were there until afterwards.'

Stephen Lowe told me how pleased he was with the reaction of the audiences, 'You never quite know what impact a piece is going to have when you write it. But you dream that one day you'll come up with a show that moves people, makes them laugh, gets people on their feet at the end and encourages them to bring their relatives. And, for me, this has been it.' Stephen thanked me for helping to publicise the production, which had led to many football fans turning out to enjoy it.

I lost count of the number of times I went to see the play. But I remember being part of the standing ovation at the first performance, a special preview on 3 June 2005, and the audience rose again to cheer and applaud at the official opening a few days later. The play's finale left a lump in the throat, a tear in the eye, and fans in awe. Just as the Great Man himself did.

10

Overpaid and Under-Talented

Whenever the anniversary of Cloughie's retirement is marked in newspapers or magazines, the focus is usually on his final couple of Premier League matches. But there were further games that he oversaw before finally saying goodbye to his managerial career.

In the 1993 County Cup Final, Clough's Forest side faced their rivals from across the River Trent, Notts County. One of the archive recordings I found included Cloughie reflecting on those last few weeks in management. He told a radio programme what he remembered of that County Cup victory, 'It was a very emotional night for me. I thought I'd finished with the league games and I'd forgotten about the County Cup. Of course, I made a hash of getting relegated. Obviously, nobody likes getting relegated – particularly me – but I justified it a fraction by taking our old enemies to town and winning 3-0. It softened the blow a wee bit.'

However, not even that trophy win was Cloughie's final match in charge. A reserve game against Stoke City was still to be played and Clough wanted to watch it. His desire to see the next crop of players coming through was as strong as ever. My friend Chris Ellis, a lifelong Forest fan, remembers being there that night and waiting outside in the Main Stand car park to see Cloughie after the match.

'At the time, his office looked out into the car park, but the windows were really high,' said Chris, who was still at school at the time. He was the youngest among a group of about six people who had gathered outside the City Ground. 'We waited and waited,' recalled Chris. 'One of the other people who was waiting had a ladder and he put the ladder against the wall of the Main Stand and looked in. He confirmed that Cloughie was still inside with a few other people.' A club representative appeared and told the group that Brian was aware they were waiting.

'I think we waited for about two hours and suddenly a side door opened and we were allowed in.'

Chris told me that, despite the curtain coming down on Clough's incredible 18-year reign at the City Ground, the mood in his office that night was relaxed and happy. 'There was a handful of people in his office and he was absolutely lovely,' said Chris, who was wearing his pin-striped Forest shirt at the time. 'He kissed us all on the cheek and let us have a photograph with him.'

Fortunately, in this pre-smartphone era Chris's mum Geraldine had already rushed home to get a camera. The next day, she paid extra to have 'Express One-Hour Processing' instead of the £3.99 four-day processing option. 'I know, it seems crazy now that you had to pay and wait four days for your photographs to be printed,' laughed Chris. 'Mum paid for the one-hour processing and came into school during the lunch break to show me the photo.' There was huge relief all round because you never knew until the photo was printed and collected from the shop that it had turned out clearly and wasn't blurred. Thankfully, the picture of Chris with Cloughie came out well. 'I put the photo in a frame and it's still a cherished possession,' he said.

* * *

After a period away from football, Cloughie was back watching live matches and became a regular visitor to Eton Park, the home of Burton Albion before they moved to the Pirelli Stadium in 2005, where son Nigel was manager. During a visit in December 2003, he watched Burton play in an FA Cup tie against Hartlepool, the club which launched his own managerial career. Cloughie sat in the stand with his wife Barbara and other son Simon alongside him. His then five-year-old grandson William was a mascot. An archive recording illustrated how much Cloughie enjoyed the experience, 'I've got my wife on my arm, my son in the dug-out and my grandson on my knee. What better Sunday afternoon could you ask for?' Referring to Barbara's rare appearance at a football match, he added, 'She's now kicking me during the match as well as getting me out of bed each morning.'

In the days leading up to the televised tie, which Burton lost 1-0, Brian and Nigel posed with the FA Cup at a local school. Brian was asked whether Burton would win and whether he had any tips for Nigel. He responded, 'Anyone can win in the FA Cup. That's the magic of it. The good, the bad and the ugly can beat the rich, the famous and the talented. And the only tip I give Nigel is, "Get off the M1 when it's foggy."'

Even though his appetite for watching football was as strong as ever, he admitted there were far too many live matches shown on television. 'Even I get sick of it – and I'm a fanatic,' he said. The number of televised games was so high during the week that he needed a rest from it, 'I have been known to doze off in the last six to nine months. My wife says it's my age, but it's not. I lose interest in it because it's at saturation point.'

Yet during one of the phone-ins I listened back to, Cloughie also admitted that he'd been wrong to predict that attendances at games would fall due to television coverage. 'Once again, I was shouting my mouth off far too early because I thought television would kill the gates – and it hasn't. They're getting better gates now than they've ever had,' he said. However, he warned that if the TV deals started to disappear or attendances began to drop, so would players' wages. 'I'm not saying they're not worth it. They're worth what they can get because we were by far underpaid as players,' he added. Forty pounds a week was his highest wage as a player, he said. 'I didn't get any £100,000 signing-on fees or anything like that.'

Then came a lovely exchange between Brian and Nigel, who was with him in the studio. Listening back intently, I could sense it was father and son enjoying each other's company and clearly thinking on the same wavelength, with some gentle humour between them.

BC, 'I started off in my national service on a pound a week.'

NC, 'And that was too much.'

BC, 'Well, some people said that as well – and he was the chairman.'

NC, 'Overpaid.'

BC, 'Overpaid and under-talented. As I say, it'll all find its own level.'

Years later, Nigel was asked about the types of things in modern football that would have annoyed his dad – including the amount of money in the game and how it is spent. 'You haven't got long enough for what would annoy him,' Nigel told talkSPORT in May 2017. 'There's a lot. I think the amount of money in football at the moment he would consider to be obscene, and the fact that there's young players who are millionaires who haven't kicked a football in the first teams and things like that.'

Brian would not have had much regard for clubs who tried to buy their way to success, 'I don't think he had much time for people who'd spend their way there, who buy titles and everything,' Nigel added. He would admire 'any manager who goes about the job in what he would consider the right way, with honesty and integrity and gets the teams to play a bit of football and work hard ... and playing for the supporters as well. Supporters get isolated a little bit because there's such a big gap now between players and supporters, and he was very keen on keeping that tight.'

The important role of supporters – and how they should be treated well by clubs, players and managers – was recalled by Cloughie during one of his radio appearances. A fan phoned the station to thank him for allowing them to touch the European Cup when Nottingham Forest had just won it in Munich in 1979. The caller, Trevor in Eastwood, admitted it was a somewhat belated 'thank you' more than 20 years after the event but he wanted to express his gratitude 'for something you won't remember, but I've never forgotten'.

Trevor explained he'd been at Munich Airport after the European Cup Final when he spotted Brian and the Forest players, along with trainer Jimmy Gordon who was carrying the trophy in a sack. 'That astonished me,' said Trevor. 'You let us have a look at the cup and touch it and I'm forever grateful.' He said he was amazed there was no security around and the trophy was being carried home in a sack. Cloughie responded, 'Well, we used to share everything, you know. That's what made us reasonably popular … We were all in it together. You'd gone to support us, we'd done you proud by winning it, why not have a look and touch of it?'

And that brings me back to the County Cup Final in 1993, the last trophy Cloughie won before his retirement. Many years later, a supporter told him how pleased they were to meet him after that momentous match. The fan told a radio programme they were among a small group which had waited patiently to see him. Eventually Brian took them into his office and – like Chris Ellis's encounter – a photograph captured the special moment. 'The photo came out brilliantly and it's now on my dining room wall,' said the fan with pride. The reply was typical Clough. 'You're not throwing rotten tomatoes at it, are you?'

Cloughie is the match summariser during a radio commentary for a match between his former sides Nottingham Forest and Derby County in September 2003. (Credit: Mike Egerton/Alamy Stock Photo)

Brian (fourth from left) with the Nottingham Forest team and assistant Peter Taylor (kneeling) at Jersey Airport in 1980. (Credit: Jersey Evening Post)

Cloughie leads a mid-morning training session on the dunes in Jersey. Ian Bowyer told me that, as far as the players were concerned, it wasn't a popular trip! (Credit: Jersey Evening Post)

Grabbing a moment with Cloughie and Garry Birtles in the radio studio for a phone-in, May 2000. (Credit: author's collection)

With the man Cloughie described as 'the Picasso of our game', John Robertson, at the launch of my first book in 2008. (Credit: author's collection)

Brian and wife Barbara on the balcony of Nottingham Council House.
(Credit: Nottingham Evening Post)

Brian at a signing session at WHSmiths before an interview with me, in which he said I made him seem better looking! (Credit: author's collection)

EXTRA SPECIAL

RUSSIAN
Precision Watches
Complete range now in stock
from 89/6 to £15/15/0

B. C. CLERKE
THE SPOT, DERBY

DAILY EXPRESS

, OCTOBER 9, 1967 PRICE 4d.

ion: for trial

RTING

Clough refuses Coventry offer

SIGNS RAMS' CONTRACT

BRIAN CLOUGH has turned down the Coventry City managership and today signed a three-year contract with Derby County.

Mr. Clough's reasons? "So corny I couldn't even begin to explain."

Assistant manager Peter Taylor also signed a three-year contract.

I understand that Coventry made Mr. Clough a massive offer to succeed Jimmy Hill. The offer, made sometime after Saturday's match against Millwall, would have involved a substantial pay rise (writes George Edwards).

GOING PLACES

Rams chairman Mr. Sam Longson commented after the contract had been signed: "I said when Brian Clough came to Derby that the big job would be to keep him here. Nothing is more certain than that Brian is going places in football, but I want him to do this with Derby County."

Mr. Clough's contract has not been altered as a result of the widespread rumours that Coventry wanted him.

"It is the same contract that has been lying in the safe for three months. It is simply that I have never got round to signing it," he said.

Naturally I was tremendously flattered by the Coventry offer. People like Don Revie and Jock Stein have been mentioned in connection with

MR. CLOUGH, accompanied by Mr. Longson, signs his contract.

Albion player joins Rams

DERBY COUNTY today signed Burton Albion's free scoring Ritchie Barker and he will be fee" and has obviously been signed because of the lack of cover in case of injuries.

he at

which alow

ntify

olice ained Hill orth, nder

d. d by tney,

?/

(20) k at Mel-

Cloughie signs a three-year contract at Derby County watched by chairman Sam Longson, October 1967. (Credit: Derby Evening Telegraph)

DERBY EVENING TELEGRAPH

INCORPORATING THE DERBY DAILY EXPRESS

No. 27,086

WEDNESDAY, JULY 24, 1968

FOR CARPETS THAT ARE REALLY CLOSE FITTED BY EXPERTS

Telephone 45524

STRAND CORNER

Assistant secretary of T.G.W.U. recommended

LABOUR'S CHIEF : NIC

SURP CHO

Iron man Dave Mackay signs for Rams

DAVE MACKAY, inspiration of Spurs and Scotland, and one of the outstanding British players of the 1960's, will lead Derby County in their bid for a Second Division revival next season (writes GEORGE EDWARDS).

He signed for the Rams in London last night after a day of talks with manager Brian Clough.

Mr. Clough, back in Derby in the early hours of this morning had a well deserved "lie in" today, but assistant manager Peter Taylor, in jubilant mood, told the story of the deal.

"Mackay was keen to stay in English football, but there was, of course, a strong possibility of him returning to Hearts.

"Brian had a long talk with him, however, and explained the job we wanted him to do at Derby.

"He agreed to sign late yesterday but, being the man he is, did not want anything made public until he had spoken to the Hearts chairman.

"He did this last night and then became a Derby County player."

MODERATE FEE

No fee was announced, but I doubt whether the Rams had to pay more than about £15,000 in all for the signature of the 33-year-old iron man of Spurs.

RAMS chairman Sydney Bradley described the deal as "a wonderful scoop for Brian Clough."

"Dave Mackay is the type of player Derby County urgently require — a born leader and just the man to fire the imagination of our supporters."

youngsters the benefit of his experience.

"There were times, last season, when our defenders were running around in circles because they did not know where and when to run. We look to Mackay to put this right."

Mackay, speaking from London, said that it was a hard decision to make because Hearts had made him a wonderful offer, but, he added:

"I am sure Derby County are going places and I am determined to help them.

"I have had nine wonderful years with Spurs, but I am not finished yet."

Mackay will not travel up to Derby until next Monday, then will leave with the Rams for Scotland on Tuesday.

The friendly against St. Johnstone, originally fixed for next Wednesday, will now be played the following day (Scottish clubs are not allowed to play public games during July) and the party will then travel back to Derby on the Friday, before playing Sunderland in a friendly at the Baseball Ground on August 3.

Mackay will therefore have an ideal opportunity to get to know his new colleagues and train with them.

Turn to page 14

NEW CALL FOR FORCE

The five-nation organisation of African Unity's Committee on Rhodesia last night renewed the African call to Britain to use force to overthrow the white regime in Salisbury.

Danny Williams fined £50 on drug charge

DANNY WILLIAMS, the singer, was arrested at his flat in Old Brompton Road, Chelsea, London, early today by Flying Squad officers and later charged with being in illegal possession of cannabis resin.

When he appeared at Marlborough Street Magistrates' Court later he was fined £50 after pleading "Guilty."

Danny Williams shot to fame with his hit recording of "Moon River."

OPIUM PIPE

Detective-sergeant John Legg told the court that police searched Williams's flat yesterday and found an opium pipe which proved to contain traces of cannabis resin.

Sergeant Legg said that Williams, a married man, was born in South Africa and came to Britain in 1961.

He earned his money by entertaining in show business but currently he was unemployed and had no income.

MR. HARRY NICHOLAS, the secretary of the Transport and General Workers' Union, was today recommended of the Labour Party.

This surprise decision taken by the national executive committee, has to be confirmed by the Labour Party conference in October before Mr. Nicholas can take up the appointment.

Mr. Nicholas reaches retiring age, 65, towards the end of next year.

Not considered

Many names of likely candidates for the post, including prominent politicians, have been publicly discussed since a sub-committee of the executive advertised the post, but Mr. Nicholas was never among them.

The favourite for the job at the end was Mr. Anthony Greenwood, Minister of Housing and Local Government and other names mentioned at various times included Mr. George Brown, Mr. Ray Gunter, Mr. Gerry Reynolds (Minister for Defence, Administration) Lord Delacourt Smith (General secretary of the Post Office Engineering Union), Mr. Alf Allen (general secretary of U.S.D.A.W.) and Mr. Vic Feather (assistant general secretary of the Trades Union Congress).

The new secretary will, in effect, be a political director with more executive power and able to play a more politically creative part than

Government supports votes at 18

VOTES for 18-year-olds is

Cloughie's signing of Dave Mackay is headline news in July 1968. (Credit: Derby Evening Telegraph)

The match report which described how Cloughie was stretchered off on Boxing Day 1962. It was an injury which effectively ended his playing career. (Credit: Sunderland Echo)

John Robertson described Clough's Forest arrival as a whirlwind – the local paper said it was a hurricane back in January 1975. (Credit: Nottingham Evening Post)

The Mirror reflects on Cloughie's retirement in 1993 by saying FA officials should hang their heads in shame for failing to make him the England boss. (Credit: Daily Mirror)

Chris Ellis was among a small group of fans invited into Cloughie's office after watching his final home match, a reserve game, at the City Ground. (Credit: Chris & Geraldine Ellis)

Cloughie reveals his Nottingham Forest Dreamteam, including Archie Gemmill who was left devastated after missing out on a place in the 1979 European Cup Final team. (Credit: Matthew Ashton / Alamy Stock Photo)

Archie Gemmill is interviewed by Gary Newbon, watched by Kenny Burns, at the unveiling of the Clough statue in Nottingham, November 2008. (Credit: Neil Hoyle)

With Archie Gemmill for the Green Jumper Podcast, 2023. (Credit: author's collection)

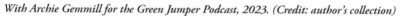

Nottingham Forest players at the unveiling of the Brian Clough statue. (Credit: Neil Hoyle)

Dad is delighted to get a picture signed by Cloughie. Yes, they did meet – as well as speaking on the radio! (Credit: author's collection)

GOAL-LINES

Send your letters to STEVE CARTER, GOAL-LINES, SHOOT! IPC Magazines Ltd, King's Reach Tower, Stamford St, London SE1 9LS. U.K. readers receive £10 for the Star Letter — £4 for every other published. Overseas readers receive a special SHOOT T-shirt. Please state which size, small, medium or large. When writing to us please mention the two features you liked best in the latest issue of SHOOT! All letters must be exclusive to SHOOT!

This week's Star Letter comes from Andrew Ogun of Lagos, Nigeria, who wins a special SHOOT T-shirt. He writes:

WE'RE NOT GOING FOR THE RIDE

★ I am writing to express my views on Ray Clemence's comments that the World Cup Finals will be devalued by having 24 Finalists.

Although I am a fan of Ray's column, in this instance I don't share his views, and I'm sure many others don't, either.

He believes that of the 24 teams, 12 will be there for the ride, which is wrong.

I know he is referring to the African and Asian teams, but let me tell you, Mr. Clemence, none of the teams from Africa is a joke.

This is supported by the fact that their system of qualifying is harder than that of the European countries, who have their qualifiers based on a League system giving each team at least two chances, whereas in Africa it is decided on a straight knockout system to enable two qualifiers from 39 nations.

So therefore no team from Asia or Africa after struggling through at least 16 matches will go to Spain in 1982 for a ride.

Mr. Clemence also thinks that African, Asian and American teams will bring down the European teams to a lower level. I don't believe this, because football standards in Europe as a whole have gone down, e.g. Malmö made the European Cup Final in 1979 and the standard of the last European Cup Final, Cup-Winners' Cup Final and European Championship leaves much to be desired from the so-called sophisticated European soccer nations.

While the European soccer fans decline in number those in Africa rise higher. For instance, in Nigeria the lower teams in Division One have crowds of 20,000, while higher teams have crowds of 45,000. They would have even more, due to the fact that most stadium capacities are 45,000 seaters.

The lowest the national team gets is 50,000, while the European teams get 100,000 fans.

I warn you, Mr. Clemence, 1982 will judge — North Korea proved it in '66, Tunisia proved it in '78 and it will also be proved in '82.

● I agree with Ray that having 24 Finalists will not be good for the World Cup. There will be even more poor games than usual — and no more good ones. I also doubt the capacity of Spain to organise a 24-team World Cup properly.

Forest boob

I THINK the Forest management pair of Clough and Taylor have made a very bad mistake in selling Ian Bowyer (above). I've been supporting Forest for five years (since they were in the Second Division) and I think he is one of the few players who has contributed so much to Forest and put in a great deal of effort into every game he's played.

If it hadn't been for Ian's experience and talented play over the last six and a half seasons then Forest wouldn't have had so much success as they have done.

I would much rather have seen Peter Ward leave Forest (who although has been given many chances has contributed about nil to Forest) especially now that Trevor Francis is back.

You may think that I'm making a mountain out of a mole-hill, but I don't think Bowyer will settle down and perform as well with Sunderland as he did at Forest.

His departure from Forest reminds me of when Clough and Taylor sold Archie Gemmill, which was another bad mistake and I think Forest fans will miss, as they did with Gemmill when he left, Ian's creative and experienced play.

I admire Brian Clough and Peter Taylor for what they've done at Forest but I also admire Ian Bowyer for the same thing.

MARCUS ALTON, LOWDHAM.

● Ian is 30 next birthday and the £250,000 Forest received represented good business.

Celtic P[ ] Scot[ ]

THERE has been [ ] recently about whi[ ] head of Ibrox, sho[ ] land's National Stad[ ] Park is finished with[ ]
There seems to be [ ] sion as Celtic Park i[ ] in fact, only alternat[ ]
I don't expect Ran[ ] with me, therefore b[ ] letters of protest, I [ ] reasons why Parkhe[ ] native to Hampden [ ] can argue with be[ ] FACTS.

1. Ibrox hasn't the [ ] even the averag[ ] Parkhead, will [ ] fans.

2. The majority of [ ] support Rangers [ ] national football t[ ] bring back the pr[ ] ers, which only st[ ] to the upsurge in [ ]

3. Ibrox could nev[ ] national stadium [ ] eliminate against [ ] the nation of Sco[ ]

4. Parkhead, unlike [ ] models invalid ce[ ]

The motto of Ra[ ] something their sta[ ] for international foo[ ]

● Over to you, Ran[ ]

Britis[ ] corr[ ]

I BELIEVE British R[ ] track with their hans[ ] drunken hooligans [ ] Wembley for [ ] England/Scotland in [ ]
When these louts [ ] repeated past war[ ] language and disgra[ ] gress light must st[ ] words.

Face facts, it must [ ] parents with young [ ] the same coaches an[ ] the B.R.'s harsh dec[ ] ing of the majority [ ]

● Of course British [ ] was killed on a train [ ] before the last gam[ ]

Pen[ ]

I'M a 15-year-old [ ] follows both Nort[ ] and British Soccer.[ ] pleased to have a p[ ] land to trade NASL[ ] couver Whitecaps.[ ] soccer souvenirs.[ ]

Petar th[ ]

My letter in Shoot! magazine (February 1981) criticising the sale of Ian Bowyer to Sunderland.

With Ian Bowyer for the Green Jumper Podcast. (Credit: author's collection)

Memorabilia from the Clough tribute play (including a photo of Colin Tarrant I took at Nottingham Playhouse) plus a glowing review of the play in The Times.

THE TIMES THURSDAY JUNE 9 2005   2WC

FIRSTNIGHT

In life or death, Clough still steals the limelight

ROBERT DAY

Theatre
The Spirit
of the Man
Nottingham Playhouse
★ ★ ★ ★ ☆
JEREMY KINGSTON

BRIAN CLOUGH was known as Old Big 'Ead, as well as the best manager the England football team never had. His fans were legion and nowhere more devoted than here, where he inspired the hitherto frail team at Nottingham Forest to scale the football heights: league champions in 1978; winners of the European Cup two years running.

These facts may not excite all of us, but of more immediate concern in this context is that he was a quirkily unpredictable character, gifted with quick wit and a way with words that seem to have vanished from the world of sport. Stephen Lowe makes him the centre

soaring above a simulacrum of Forest's home ground like the Buddha emerging from a lotus.

Waiting on a bench outside the heavenly showers sit D.H. Lawrence, Lord Byron and General William Booth, East Midlanders all, awaiting the call to nip back to Earth and inspire the living. Cloughie, the new arrival, is handed a message that says "forest" and "lost" and descends by celestial lift, only to find himself stuck with a would-be playwright lost in Sherwood Forest.

So far so good, and whenever Colin Tarrant's Clough is dishing out the advice, with football his guide at all times, the fun is tremendous.

Tarrant has turned himself into an astonishingly lifelike re-

FIRSTNIGHT
in **T2**
■ The Ballet Boyz

semblance of the original. The widow's peak and dense eyebrows are easy to re-create, as is that odd habit of wobbling his head around as though uncertain of his neck. But Tarrant also catches the nasal voice, almost a whine, the often expressionless face and the rapid delivery of the lines Lowe gives him.

Seen and heard only by the neurotic playwright — Ken Bradshaw is required to play him as a hysteric with a capital H — Clough helps him to finish his Robin Hood drama, although what we see of it looks frightful. Tarrant plays the camp actor cast as the leader of the Merry Men, and Robin too, but the sad fact is that none of the backstage mishaps are remotely as interesting as the Clough character.

Jamie Vartan's design delightfully turns a bank of showers into Robin's mighty oak, and the players are marshalled effectively enough by Alan Dossor. But it is Tarrant's Clough

Brian with Kenny Burns at the City Ground, September 2003. (Credit: author's collection)

A letter from Cloughie telling Forest fan and injured soldier Billy Lundy to 'get up off your backside' and get to the City Ground. (Credit: B. Lundy)

Nottingham Forest Football Club

City Ground
Nottingham NG2 5FJ
Telephone 868336
Information Desk 860232
Pools Office 864808

Telegrams
Forestball Nottingham

Manager:
Brian Clough

Secretary/Treasurer:
Ken Smales

Ref :- BC/MJD

15th February, 1979

Guardsman William Lundy,
Burns Unit,
Woolwich Hospital,
London, S.E.18

Dear Bill,

This letter might come as a surprise to you and it will be an even bigger surprise when I tell you to get up off your backside and get yourself fit, because there are a lot of games to be played at the City Ground this season and I have a seat waiting for you for all the matches for the rest of the season as soon as you are able to come and see us. I know it is difficult for you and I won't pretend to begin to understand how you feel, but you know we want you here just as soon as possible.

We all hope you get better quickly and everyone here sends their love and best wishes. We are all thinking of you and looking forward to seeing you at one of Nottingham Forest's matches when you are well.

Kind regards.

Yours sincerely,

B. Clough,
Manager.

The Daily Mirror reports Brian is confident Derby can win the title in 1972.

Clough declares his admiration of Arsene Wenger, a cutting I took to the Emirates Stadium during a tour behind the scenes.

Greek champions for Euro Reds

By JOHN LAWSON

AEK ATHENS, the team managed by Ferenc Puskas, are Nottingham Forest's glamour opponents in the second round of the European Cup.

And the Reds, delighted with the draw after beating Liverpool this week, are no strangers to the Greek champions, having drawn 1-1 in Athens in a pre-season friendly.

GLAMOUR

When news of the draw in Zurich reached the City Ground, manager Brian Clough beamed: "That suits us fine. They are a big club, play good football and with Puskas as their manager, they have no shortage of glamour.

"There will be tremendous interest out there in the tie. When we played them in a pre-season game it got really big billing."

And the Forest chief quipped: "I hope they make more noise in the hotel than they did when we were out there

BRIAN CLOUGH — beamed when he heard the news.

Clark faces test

VETERAN Frank Clark remained the centre of attention at the City Ground today as Nottingham Forest prepared for their trip to Aston Villa. The 35-year-old full back earned considerable praise for his effective return to the Reds' defence in their European Cup triumph at Liverpool in midweek. But injuries sustained in that match could

Cuttings from 1978, Forest's first European Cup match on foreign soil. (Credit: Nottingham Post)

Glory in Greece!

JOHN LAWSON'S exclusive file on the stars of AEK

EVEN[I]
EU[I]
SP[I]

Seeking lost Greek pride

"HEEZ GOOD, YEH?" screamed the voice of a man sitting in front of the English section of the Press Box at the New Philadelphia Stadium in Athens a fortnight ago.

On a night when there was very little to cheer the Greek locals, at least one man got some pleasure in every single shout and shot from THOMAS MAV-ROS.

It was as if he wanted the English journalists to go back home confident

Coverage of the launch of my first book (Credit: Nottingham Post), alongside John McGovern at a signing session. (author's collection)

Legend's book signing proves a big draw

We still worship you, Cloughie!

By SIMON ATKINSON

HUNDREDS of fans queued up to catch a glimpse of Nottingham Forest legend Brian Clough — at a supermarket.

The former Reds boss visited the Asda store in West Bridgford to sign copies of his new autobiography, *Walking On Water*.

And the queue to meet him snaked through the store and out into the sun-drenched car park.

As a trembling David Harris walked away from the table to pay for his freshly autographed book, he joked: "I can't even sign the credit card slip. I'm 37 years old and my hands are shaking! I've met my hero, a masterful, awesome, genius."

First in the queue were 24-year-old Sarah Clarke and partner Marcus Alton, 35, both of Gedling, who were outside the store at 6.50am — over an hour before Asda opened.

Their patience was rewarded when Cloughie signed their copies and handed over a bottle of champagne.

Referring to his drinking, featured in the book and reported in the *Post*, Cloughie laughed and told the pair: "I used to like a glass in the bath. It's easy to have a drink to celebrate a win, but when we lost, I'd drown my sorrows."

Sarah said: "There was no way I was going to miss this. I'm a huge fan of Clough and was born in '78 when they won the European Cup.

Meeting Cloughie at a book signing at Asda, West Bridgford, in 2002.
Main photo credit: Nottingham Post.

Interviewing Nigel Clough at an event to include Brian in the Hall of Fame at the National Football Museum. (Credit: author's collection)

11

'Get Off Your Backside'

It must have been an emotional encounter.

A dying man had been asked what he would like to do in his final days. 'I'd like to meet Brian,' was the reply.

The man's wife, who had asked the question, then made arrangements for Cloughie to visit her husband in hospital.

'I went into the hospital and we chatted,' recalled Brian, who went on to say that the man had difficulty talking due to cancer affecting his throat. The conversation was conducted through his wife who explained what her husband was trying to say.

Just as Brian was about to leave, the man conveyed a message to his special visitor. He said there had been one thing in particular that had upset him that year. 'I thought he was going to say it was about me,' said Brian, 'or the fact I'd retired. But no. He told me he'd got his season ticket for Derby and he couldn't use it up.

'I said to him, "I'll see you in a few weeks."' The reply was, 'If you're lucky.'

Brian continued, 'I said to him, "Aye, there's only one lucky bloke here – and that's me. If you're lucky, you'll see me in a few weeks."'

Listening back to Brian telling that story during a visit to BBC Radio Derby, I could only imagine the effect his surprise appearance must have had in the hospital that day. It's the type of scenario you'd expect to see in a tear-jerking movie about a man's last request. But this was for real – and was only being revealed because listeners had voted Brian the most influential local person in the past 30 years.

As Brian sat in the radio studio talking to presenter John Holmes, the memory of that visit to Derby City Hospital had been prompted by a woman who had phoned the radio station to pay her own tribute in relation to a similar experience.

That caller, from Alvaston in Derby, had described how she met Brian in the city hospital some years before, when her husband was very ill.

'He [Brian] came in and sat on his bed and talked to him and cheered him up,' she said. 'He really made him laugh. My husband was 54 at the time and Brian said, "Now then, young man, how are you?" Then he said, "I feel bu**ered – I could just get in there with you."'

'I've never forgotten how nice Brian was,' said the caller. At that point, John Holmes made a point of highlighting how important this 'personal touch' was – and the effect on the people involved, 'These things go such a long way, don't they?'

'Yes, they do,' said the woman, who was clearly very pleased to be able to pass on her personal thanks to Brian, as part of this special broadcast.

From the various conversations I've had with people who knew Cloughie well, I can safely say that these were just two of many examples of how he went out of his way to help others in need, away from the glare of publicity.

Perhaps one of his more unusual goodwill gestures involved a soldier who had been badly injured while serving in Northern Ireland and was lying in hospital. As well as offering him a regular ticket for the remaining matches at the City Ground, Clough gave the soldier the type of order that only he could get away with, 'Get up off your backside.'

The soldier was Grenadier Guard and Forest fan Billy Lundy, who had lived close to the City Ground and, wherever he was posted, always put his Forest scarf and photos on display next to his bed. It reminded him of home.

Billy was on foot patrol in Northern Ireland during the Troubles in early 1979 when a device inside a car exploded as he walked by. Seriously injured, including almost 40 per cent third degree burns, Billy was airlifted to the military wing of Musgrave Park Hospital in Belfast. From there, he was flown to a specialist burns unit at a military hospital in London. It was while he was being treated in the capital that the unexpected letter arrived.

Billy told me, 'When I was injured, I didn't return to my base, so my mates had to take down all my Forest stuff from the wall, put it in my suitcase and send it on to me. They obviously knew I was a big Forest fan so they had the idea of writing to Brian Clough to see if he would write a letter to a Forest fan who'd been injured in Northern Ireland. And he did.'

The envelope was addressed to Billy Lundy, C/O the Burns Unit, Woolwich Hospital, London. As Billy's hands were badly burned, a nurse opened the letter, dated 13 February 1979, and read it to him. This is what it said:

Dear Bill, this letter may come as a surprise to you, and it will be an even bigger surprise when I tell you to get up off your backside and get yourself fit, because there are a lot of games to be played at the City Ground this season and I have a seat waiting for you for all the matches for the rest of the season as soon as you're able to come and see us. I know it is difficult for you and I won't pretend to begin to understand how you feel, but you know we want you here just as soon as possible.

We all hope you get better quickly and everyone here sends their love and best wishes. We are all thinking of you and looking forward to seeing you at one of Nottingham Forest's matches when you are well.

Kind regards,
Yours sincerely
B. Clough,
Manager.

The letter, on Nottingham Forest-headed paper, was personally signed by Cloughie. Billy was almost lost for words when the nurse showed him who had signed it.

'My friends came to visit me in hospital and they couldn't believe it,' said Billy. 'Nobody else could have written a letter like that. You can hear his voice when you read it. They're his words. I don't think anybody else other than Brian Clough would have told me to get off my backside.'

It was a privilege to speak to Billy on the *Green Jumper* podcast. And I must thank him for kindly allowing me to include a copy of the letter in this book. He took Cloughie's message in the spirit it was intended. 'I thought it was quite funny because my backside was badly burned and I was doing my best to keep off it in the first place,' he told me.

Talking to Billy, I was in awe of a modesty which belied the tremendous courage he had shown as a soldier. He decided not to take Cloughie up on his offer of a seat at the City Ground. 'I thought that would be very rude of me,' he said. When Billy was well enough, he did eventually return to watch Forest at the City Ground and also saw them lift the European Cup in Madrid. 'I was just very pleased with the letter he sent me and I left it at that. It's something I will always cherish.'

Another cherished letter from Cloughie was written when he was still a player, long before his managerial miracles. But it came at a time when he was facing an uncertain future, having suffered the terrible injury which effectively ended his playing career.

Trevor Moore, who was an avid Middlesbrough fan, had grown up close to Ayresome Park and wrote to Brian after his injury while playing for Sunderland on Boxing Day 1962. Trevor's dad, Fred, had been a director at Middlesbrough and was also well-known as a local councillor. After Fred had written to Brian, saying his son would love to meet him, Cloughie called at their home – but ironically Trevor was out playing football with his mates. Just imagine that! Brian Clough arrives at your house to meet you – and you're not there to greet him. But the next best thing was to receive a personal letter. That's what Trevor received in February 1963. Typed and personally signed, it read:

Dear Trevor,

Thank you for your letter, it was kind of you to write to me. I remember coming round to see you but it doesn't seem as long as two and a half years. My injury is coming along fine but I still have my leg in plaster. I hope it won't be too long before I'm playing football again. Give my regards to your father.

Yours sincerely,

Brian Clough

The letter is now being kept safely for posterity by Trevor's daughter, Sam. Trevor, who passed away in 2019, had fixed it inside the front cover of one of Brian's autobiographies. 'Whenever we went to see my dad he would show us the letter, he was absolutely over the moon about it,' Sam told me. 'He treasured it all his life. Dad said Brian was the best centre-forward he had ever seen and was obviously the greatest manager there's ever been. He also liked watching his television appearances, with those outspoken and controversial views. On the day Brian called round at his house and he was out, he said it was just his luck and that it could only happen to him. He idolised Brian.'

Sam incorporated the story of the letter in a musical production of her dad's life, called *Our Trevor*. She also told me about an occasion when her dad was waiting outside Ayresome Park to get Brian's autograph. A young boy was among the crowd and started shouting 'Cloughie, Cloughie' to get the attention of Boro's star striker. Clough was surrounded by fans and turned around. Pointing to the young lad he said, 'It's Mr Clough to you.' Sam laughs at the memory, 'That was typical Brian Clough.'

Many years later, her dad having sadly passed away, Sam travelled to the City Ground to watch her beloved Middlesbrough play Nottingham Forest. She knew it was something Trevor would have wanted her to do. Watching the footage of Cloughie on the big screens before the teams appeared, Sam was soon gripped by emotion, 'I'd never seen that footage, it was amazing. The European Cup wins and those glory years. It was very emotional because I knew what it had meant to my dad. I felt he was with me that night, it was like he was standing with me.'

Sometimes, only football can generate those special feelings you never forget.

12

A Box of Matches

Football directors – and chairmen in particular – were often a target for Cloughie during his media interviews. I listened back to a recording of one of his radio appearances in 2002 and he was as sharp as a tack when referring to directors who knew nothing about the game, 'The only match they've seen is in a box of Swan Vestas.'

Yet despite his much-publicised clashes with chairmen over the years (Derby's Sam Longson and Ernie Ord at Hartlepools being prime examples), it may come as a surprise to know that he had very cordial relationships with various directors. He was even bubbling with praise for the chairman of his former club, Middlesbrough.

A comment made by one of his old chairmen gives a better insight into that contrast in opinions, 'His private persona was very different to his public persona. He was a very kind and considerate man.' Those remarks came from the former Nottingham Forest chairman, Brian Appleby QC, in an interview with the BBC's Mark Shardlow in 2019. Mr Appleby, who died in 2021, was on the Forest committee when Clough arrived at the City Ground, and he became chairman during Brian's early days with the Reds. 'We were doing very badly and we were going downhill,' he said. 'Brian Clough was a very controversial figure and a lot of the committee didn't want him to come. I think they were frightened of what would happen. My view was that we can't be any worse than we are now and we need a breath of fresh air. That is exactly what Brian Clough was.'

Mr Appleby said they enjoyed a very good working relationship and even watched cricket together at Trent Bridge. Clough described the lawyer, who later became a judge, as one of the nicest directors he had worked with. In the 2019 interview, the former Forest chairman described how his wife had been 'terrified' at the thought of meeting Clough because she feared he was a formidable character. 'Within about an hour she was eating out of his hand and she thought he was lovely,' he said. 'My little boy, who was about five or six, was out on the lawn playing football with him.' He went on to say how he kept in touch with Brian for many years, 'I liked him. It's as simple as that. I liked the man and I respected him.' Clough's generosity was described as incredible, 'My son [Jonathan] was going away to boarding school and was very unhappy about it. And he told Clough. He took Jonathan to the dressing room and asked him who his favourite player was. Jonathan said Trevor Francis and Clough got Trevor Francis out of the bath and said, "Give Jonathan your shirt, son." And he gave him his number nine shirt. He wrote to him at school. That was the real Brian Clough.'

During the interview, Mark suggested that not all club chairmen could deal with Clough's public persona – especially Sam Longson at Derby. Their disagreements contributed to Clough and his assistant Peter Taylor resigning from their positions at the Baseball Ground. 'I think the trouble was that Sam Longson thought he could control Brian Clough totally,' said Mr Appleby. 'My attitude with Brian was, "Let him get on with it, he knows what he's doing." I always used to tell the story in my after-dinner speech that I had no problem with Brian. He did exactly what I told him to do, because I saw him every day and I told him, "Do whatever you like, Brian." And he did.'

* * *

A crucial half an hour in Nottingham Forest's history involved committee member Stuart Dryden, who subsequently became a close friend of Cloughie. It happened during the evening of New Year's Day, 1975. At the Post House Hotel near the M1 at Sandiacre, between Nottingham and Derby, Dryden met Clough to discuss the final arrangements for his appointment as the new Forest manager. Following the previous night's revelries, the hotel was virtually deserted, apart from a couple of bar staff. 'They showed a lot of curiosity in Brian, because they recognised him of course; but they had no idea who I was,' Dryden told the *Nottingham Evening Post* in a cutting I found from 2003, marking ten years since Brian's departure from the City Ground. 'We sat there for half an hour and finalised it all.'

I was fascinated to discover that Clough had first been approached by Dryden back in 1973, when he was a new arrival on the club's committee. On that occasion, Brian had decided to go to Brighton & Hove Albion, apparently after reading in a national newspaper that the Forest chairman, Jim Wilmer, had said he was going to take three weeks seeking 'the right man'. But by the time 1975 arrived, Brian had survived for only 44 days at Leeds and felt ready to return to the game. Dryden initially met Clough in Derby and then things moved very quickly. 'I was in a much stronger position than I had been in 1973,' said Dryden. With Forest struggling in the Second Division, the majority of the club's committee had agreed that Allan Brown had to go. Dryden spearheaded Forest's second attempt to lure Clough. 'After I got an indication that Brian would be interested in the job, I was able to go back to Nottingham and do some quick lobbying among the committee,' he said. Within 24 hours, Dryden was confident that the majority of the committee would vote in favour of appointing Clough.

After their meeting at the Post House, Dryden drove back to his house in Nottingham, along what is now Brian Clough Way, seemingly unaware of just how momentous that 30-minute discussion would be, 'I just nurtured the fond hope that, at some time in the next five years, we would gain promotion from the Second Division.' But the next five years saw success beyond all expectations. Dryden would be alongside Clough at a parks pitch in Nottingham to watch England's first £1m player make his Forest debut in a third-team match against Notts County. That same player, Trevor Francis, would score the winning goal to secure the first of two successive European Cups.

Clough never forgot Dryden's help in securing the Forest job. When the subpostmaster was accused of dishonesty in connection with the Post Office he ran in Nottinghamshire, Brian remained loyal to his friend. Clough's appreciation of Dryden's efforts to champion his case among other members of the Forest committee was clear when he reflected on the life of his late friend some years later, 'Dear Stuart ... we were to share many fabulous times together after he became chairman, and we became the best of friends. He was a good man, a loyal man, whose dignity and support never wavered. Nor did my regard for him when, after being found guilty of some fraud at his Post Office, he was sent to prison. Poor man! I did what I could, but how can you help in circumstances like that?'

Clough went on to say that he hoped his loyalty to Dryden at such a difficult time was as comforting as the faith and friendship he had always extended to Brian, 'The success I was to achieve on behalf of Forest would not have been possible without Stuart Dryden's support.'

That's not to say Dryden didn't challenge Clough if there was a good reason to do so. Take, for example, the free transfer of a midfielder to Manchester United in Brian's early days at the City Ground. He wanted to offload Tommy Jackson and allowed him to join Tommy Docherty at Old Trafford for nothing. Brian recalled, 'There was concern at Forest when I made the decision to release him without a fee. Stuart Dryden came to see me and said, "You have let Jackson go for nothing and he's been snapped up by Manchester United?" He was obviously suggesting that anybody signed by United *must* be good or at least be worth a transfer fee.' Clough replied in no uncertain terms that he didn't care if Jackson had signed for Real Madrid. 'He can't play,' Brian insisted. Jackson may not have fitted into Clough's plans but he certainly proved he could play, winning 35 international caps for Northern Ireland. Dryden might just have had a point. Thankfully, Clough worked his magic with other players who were already on Forest's books, namely John Robertson, Martin O'Neill, Tony Woodcock, Viv Anderson and Ian Bowyer.

* * *

When it comes to the category of chairmen and directors who were liked by Cloughie, there's no way that the Hartlepools chairman, Ernie Ord, would sit comfortably in that select group of individuals. However, Ord's successor would no doubt be allowed to relax in a nice comfy chair in a prime position. Not only did John Curry get on really well with Brian, but he received some crucial help from him when he needed it the most.

In his autobiography, Clough put it simply, 'Ernie Ord annoyed me.' The main cause of this annoyance was his 'interference in my job'. When Curry took over, things were different. Clough could get on with the task at hand and was generally supported behind the scenes by Curry, who was the leader of the Conservative group on the local council. He was willing to back Clough in the signing of several players, driving down to Nottinghamshire to join a meeting with them and helping to get the deals agreed. When Clough and Taylor left Hartlepools to join Derby County, they presented Curry with a farewell gift. The inscription on the lighter read, 'If we stay in the game another 100 years, we will not find another chairman as good as you.'

Having put his heart and soul into turning around the club's fortunes, even visiting working men's clubs and persuading supporters to reach into their pockets and donate cash, it's understandable that Clough was initially reluctant to leave Hartlepools. The author Chris Hull, who wrote the book *Alchemy* about Clough and Taylor's time at the club, said Brian felt the job wasn't finished, 'He'd managed to raise the money to keep the club going and then it didn't sit right with him to then say, "I'm leaving."'

Chris told me that it would have been difficult for Clough to tell Curry he was going to Derby. But it didn't take long for Taylor to persuade his mate to leave. 'Taylor couldn't get out fast enough,' said Hull. The club was being left in a better

119

position than when they arrived and the offer to work at Derby was too good to turn down. But even at Derby, Clough's appreciation of Curry's support meant that he would still do all he could when he heard his former club was in trouble. Hull told me that Curry phoned the Derby boss and explained that Hartlepool – as they were renamed following Clough and Taylor's exit – were in dire straits. He asked whether Brian would buy one of their players to help generate some much-needed cash. 'I think it was [for] a tax demand, something that needed to be paid very quickly,' said Hull. Derby bought Tony Parry and Hartlepool were saved. 'I think that was repaying a favour to John Curry,' said Hull.

* * *

Staying in the north-east – and Clough was full of praise for the Middlesbrough chairman, Steve Gibson, when he appeared on a radio programme in March 2004. Brian's hometown club had just won the League Cup after beating Bolton Wanderers 2-1 at the Millennium Stadium in Cardiff. 'I'm absolutely thrilled and delighted for everybody up there,' he said. Sitting next to his former Nottingham Forest defender Kenny Burns, Clough added, 'For Middlesbrough to win something after about 120 years, well, I was as much thrilled for them as when I was with Kenneth Burns and we were winning things.'

Brian described Gibson as 'an absolute fanatic' and 'a bubbly young man'. He was impressed with his total commitment to Boro. 'He put his cash in and didn't really want it on the front page. People have joined football clubs for the wrong reasons in the last 20 years – they wanted their photographs on the front page of the newspapers. They weren't footballing people. I used to work for a lot of them. But Gibson is a fanatic. He's put his money in, he's never asked for it back and he got as much pleasure as anybody out of Middlesbrough winning that cup.'

The subject of Middlesbrough qualifying for Europe also came up during the discussion. 'Anybody gets into Europe nowadays,' said Brian. 'You can even get into the European Cup if you finish fourth in the league, which I find absolutely ridiculous.' Asked whether he thought the Middlesbrough manager Steve McClaren was a good coach, Brian said he thought he was. 'He's got his feet on the floor, having been the assistant at Manchester United. He's now working for a living, because anybody can be second-in-command at Manchester United.' Cloughie added that even the presenter of the radio programme could be the assistant at Old Trafford – 'and that's saying something!'

* * *

When Cloughie had to serve a three-month touchline ban, after clobbering a couple of supporters who had run on to the pitch after the final whistle of the League Cup quarter-final against Queens Park Rangers in 1989, he ended-up sitting among the club's directors. For Brian, that was punishment enough. The mere thought of having to sit in the directors' box 'with directors and directors' wives' always sent a chill down his spine. However, he once wrote that during his ban from the dugout, one of the Forest directors, Jimmy Pell, 'had the pleasure of my company'. Brian described Jimmy as a dear friend and a lovely man. I had the pleasure of Jimmy's company when I met him while researching one of my books. Sadly, he's no longer with us, but I sat enthralled as he recounted stories of the times he spent with Brian. He was proud to show me a miniature replica of the European Cup, made from Waterford glass, that Cloughie had given him as a souvenir.

'Brian Clough was a very generous man,' Jimmy told me. 'Whenever I had a charity to support and needed a financial donation, he would always arrange to do a newspaper article for me and make sure that the cheque from the newspaper went straight to the charity concerned.'

Jimmy had been elected on to the Forest board just a few months after Brian's arrival. Being a part of the incredible success over the next five years was a dream come true. Cloughie even bought some red roses for Jimmy's mum, so she could put them in a glass vase which had been specially commissioned for one of Forest's cup successes.

When Jimmy was elected as vice-chairman, he would have regular contact with Cloughie. He recalled, 'But when he used to phone me at the office, he would say, "It's Brian here," and I would reply, "Brian who?" just to pull his leg!

'On one occasion he phoned me before we were due to play in the UEFA Cup against Celtic at the City Ground. It was a night match and during the day it had been bitterly cold. Brian rang me and said, "Get down here."

'"What's the matter, Brian?" I asked him.

'He said, "We've got problems with the Spanish referee."

'"Well, what can I do about it?" I asked.

'"Get down here," he insisted.

'So I went down to the ground and the Spanish referee was inspecting the pitch. It was freezing, even in the middle of the afternoon, and I was wearing a sheepskin coat. All the Celtic fans were parked up in buses near the ground and there was no way we could cope with about 12,000 Celtic supporters going rampant in Nottingham. Clough came out to the side of the pitch and said, "It's all right, we can play in this."

'But the referee was looking very doubtful. Eventually, the UEFA representative turned up and he was from Finland – it was almost like a summer's day to him. So the game went ahead.

'After the second leg, we flew back from Glasgow to East Midlands Airport in a small plane called a Fokker Friendship. But Brian didn't like the look of it and refused to get on. Anyway, we managed to persuade him – and I told him, "It's OK Brian, once we're flying, it's all downhill, so it won't be too bad!"'

Another of Jimmy's stories involved a trip to Spain, when he was lucky enough to be one of the few people, besides the players, to be invited by Clough, 'I'll never forget being with him the day we were promoted to the old First Division back in 1977. Clough had booked 22 places for a break in Cala Millor in Majorca. We were due to fly out there as Bolton were playing Wolves. We'd completed all our matches and were third in the division. Bolton required at least a point against Wolves to keep their hopes alive.

'We arrived at East Midlands Airport at half past two ... I was the only director invited by Clough on this occasion. The flight took off at three o'clock, with an announcement from the captain, "I'm very pleased to welcome on board the Nottingham Forest team." Then at 3.20pm, while we were in the air, we heard that Bolton were losing 1-0. We knew that if that continued, Forest would be promoted. But then we went out of radio contact and couldn't follow the score.

'We arrived in Palma and I phoned home. My mum said, "Something's happened to Forest," but she didn't know the full details. Eventually, Cloughie managed to phone home and it was confirmed that we were promoted. We stayed in Cala Millor and at about two o'clock in the morning, John McGovern and I went out to get 22 packets of fish and chips to celebrate.

'The next day, I was relaxing in the sunshine when Clough and Taylor came up to me and said, "You've got promoted now. It better be Shilton, Gemmill and Burns before we kick off the new season." I felt like I was sitting in quicksand! Just the thought of it! But of course we signed Peter Shilton, Archie Gemmill and Kenny Burns before Christmas and we went on to win the championship.'

While Cloughie disliked sitting in the directors' box during the touchline ban, he admitted that sitting next to Jimmy had made it bearable – but only just. 'The problem is he [Jimmy] talks incessantly through matches,' he said. 'Sitting near him, I learned that his fridge was working perfectly, that his dog was regular and that he was eating and sleeping well himself. Aye, the quality of the conversation was top notch.' But he added that Jimmy *did* make him laugh – and that's a precious gift.

Funnily enough, when I spoke to Jimmy his recollections of sitting alongside Brian were slightly different. 'I remember that when he got a touchline ban, he sat next to me in the directors' box,' said Jimmy. 'He was shouting and bellowing at the players – I thought it was best to sit there and say nothing!'

And that brings me nicely to another one of Cloughie's classic quotes that I discovered while researching this book. He'd retired by this time and was talking about a forthcoming Derby v Forest match. He was asked how he thought it would go. Skilfully sidestepping the question, he replied, 'The only problem I've got is deciding which board of directors to sit with – because they're all bums!'

13

Split Loyalties

To put it mildly, Brian Clough was not known for his diplomacy. That's why people loved to hear him in radio interviews or watch him on TV. You never knew what he was going to say next – and who he was about to upset! But when it came to the issue of 'Derby or Forest?' he was more than a match for the finest of diplomats.

Both clubs remained close to his heart, even though the circumstances of his departures from them were far from perfect. One of his biggest regrets was resigning from Derby after a boardroom row. At Forest, relegation in his final season left him feeling 'ashamed', despite the unprecedented success he had brought the club.

A magazine article in 2004 asked him the question, 'Where does your heart lie: Derby or Forest?' He said he was split between the two. 'I spent one third of my life up until 1993 at Forest and fulfilled everything I ever wanted in management. At Derby, I was young, full of myself and that side I left behind in 1973 was the best I ever managed.'

Just a few months before that article, he was asked on a radio programme whether – as Forest manager – he had ever felt the same passion as the fans on derby day. The answer, as I listened back to the cassette tape, was instant. 'I wish I could have stuck ten past Derby,' he said. 'My loyalty was total. Over the top was my loyalty to Forest.' And he didn't stop there. Referring to an anti-aircraft gun he used during his national service, he added, 'If I'd have had a Bofors gun on Trent Bridge, the Derby coach wouldn't have left the Baseball Ground.' That would certainly have been over the top.

Asked how he thought a forthcoming Forest v Derby match would play out, his answer would have prompted the Diplomatic Service to consider signing a new recruit with the initials BHC. His main wish, he said, was for it to be a good match that was a credit to both sides. The radio station 106 Century FM engineered quite a coup when they arranged for Cloughie to be their match summariser for the derby at the City Ground in September 2003. Fans of the Reds and the Rams were united in their applause when he walked into the stadium for a pre-match interview. He told Century, 'I don't come back here very often, but the response of the fans has been incredible.'

Clough had arrived 40 minutes before kick-off and initially waited in the reception area of the club he once ruled from top to bottom. He was then greeted by his fellow summariser, former Reds star Kenny Burns. My photographs of Brian's visit that day are still some of my favourites. There's also a picture of him in the commentary box, which I've included in this book. During the match, which ended in a draw, he told listeners, 'It's a bit dull at the moment and it needs someone to set it on fire.' But when the commentator Darren Fletcher said he was enjoying the company so much that he wanted to sit back and listen to Clough and Burns, the Master Manager replied in typical fashion, 'It wouldn't do you any harm at all!'

His stint as a match summariser also featured one of my favourite Cloughie phrases, which I still repeat to this day. It came in response to an expression that I think has become a very lazy way for journalists to ask a question. Instead of asking what Brian thought about a particular subject, or what his opinion was, Cloughie was asked, 'Brian, what's your take?' There was a slight pause before the master interviewee gave his response, 'What's my take? You speak English to me, man!' Every time I hear that lazy term used in an interview, Clough's words are repeated loud and clear in my head. Maybe I'm old-fashioned. But I think he was dead right.

Away from the pressures of matchday, Cloughie's love for Derby, as a place he could call home, never wavered. In April 2001 he was voted the most influential person of the last 30 years in Derbyshire, in a poll conducted by BBC Radio Derby. During a visit to the radio station, he spoke to several fans who phoned in. The recording makes entertaining listening, especially when Chris called from Belper.

Chris, 'Good morning, Brian.'

BC, 'Chris, good morning to you. And you were christened Christopher.'

Chris, 'Well, I prefer Chris, thank you very much.'

BC, 'What were you christened?'

Chris, 'I was christened Christopher.'

BC, 'Aye, you were christened Christopher. Get on man, what do you want?'

At that point, 'Christopher' went on to say how much Brian meant to Derby County fans and suggested that if ever he wanted to return to football, there was a place for him at Pride Park. 'If I want to come back in, I'll throw my cap in the ring and the directors will decide,' was the diplomatic reply.

Brian also spoke about how he would always be associated with Derby as a city, to such an extent that he received mail which was addressed simply to 'Brian Clough, Derby'.

As a gesture of the listeners' admiration for their famous resident, the show's presenter John Holmes gave him an engraved crystal rose bowl. 'It's absolutely beautiful,' said Brian. 'I'm partial to tangerines and I'll get a dozen satsumas in this vase.' Looking at the presentation box, he said, 'Have you put it through the bomb squad? I'm not that popular, you know.' He described it as 'a miracle' to have won the vote and told one caller he had given his football medals to his grandson, adding, 'He can now retire overnight at the age of 12.'

A few years later, during another phone-in programme, he took a call from a Rams fan called Douglas. The start of the conversation was brilliant.

Douglas, 'Up the Rams, Brian.'

BC, 'How far up?'

Douglas, 'As far as you like.'

BC, 'I'm sitting surrounded by Nottingham people here, you be careful. We can all be brave on the telephone, you know. Get on, what do you want?'

Douglas, 'Why can't we win away? If we'd got three or four points away, we'd have been out of trouble.'

BC, '*If* is the biggest word in football – and in life. If my auntie had had b**ls, she'd have been my uncle.'

There's just no answer to that.

However, a little bit of digging into the archives showed that the importance of picking up points away from home was one of the first issues Cloughie highlighted in a 1967 newspaper interview. 'It is only in away matches that one can really judge a team,' he said. 'It is away from home that promotion is won and it is these matches, of course, that present the problems. Winning away is not easy.' He said he was willing to adopt what might appear to be defensive tactics in away matches, if he felt it would secure a win. The same approach might even apply at home in certain circumstances, he said. Supporters wanted a winning team and there were more ways of achieving that besides all-out attacking football.

* * *

Cloughie always cherished the football honours he won with Derby because they were his first major achievements in management. Speaking in 2002, he still believed that his best feeling of winning anything came when the Rams secured the Second Division title in 1969, 'It was the first thing I'd won and I thought to myself, "We're among the big boys now."' Along with securing the First Division championship 1972, these memories were particularly special, he said. 'It's like your first girlfriend. You never forget her, do you?'

When Derby's league title was confirmed, Cloughie was on holiday in the Scilly Isles with his family. 'I liked to go on holiday while everybody else was working,' he recalled. 'All the other managers were saying, "How do you get away with it?" I said, "It's simple, you just get on an aeroplane and go."' Derby had completed their fixtures and Leeds were the favourites to win the title, if they could draw at Wolves. A victory for Liverpool against Arsenal would have put them above the Rams on goal difference. Both results went Derby's way, with Leeds losing and Liverpool getting nothing more than a draw. 'It is obviously more of a feat for Derby to finish top than one of the big-city clubs,' said Clough at the time.

Looking back at the achievement 30 years later, Brian remembered being with his parents, wife and children at a hotel on the island of Tresco. 'I was giving the guests in the lounge a glass of champagne,' recalled Cloughie. 'One woman said, "What are we celebrating?" I said, "We've won the championship – the First Division." "Oh," she said, "which First Division is that?" I said that I worked in football for a living. She said, "Well, I'm very proud and pleased for you." And then she started reading her book.'

To mark the 40th anniversary of the league title, Brian's sons Nigel and Simon gave an interview to the *Derby Evening Telegraph* and described that memorable trip to the Scilly Isles. 'I remember the hotel was a posh place and the guests were not really football people,' said Simon. A talk on the flora and fauna of the islands had been interrupted by Brian bursting in to convey the good news to his wife Barabara, who was in the audience. Nigel said, 'Apparently, the person giving the lecture said to Dad, "That's splendid, very well done," and a few people started clapping but one woman who was sat close to Mum asked, "Who is that man and what is he talking about?" For the rest of the holiday it seemed like those who had been in the room looked daggers at us for interrupting the lecture!' Nevertheless, Brian was pleased that his parents were with him to also share the celebration.

* * *

A newspaper cutting from the *Derby Evening Telegraph* five years before that title win gave an insight into Clough's early philosophy at the Baseball Ground. The headline was 'My First Job – To Apply Basics' and the article took the form of a question-and-answer session with the newspaper's sports editor, George Edwards. Clough was asked whether he had to forget Derby's previous successes and failures and 'start from scratch'.

'I've got to,' came the reply. 'First of all, I've hardly got a long enough memory to remember many of the successes!' Clough said people spoke about past glories because there were no current successes to talk about, adding, 'It's my job to provide these successes.'

This sentiment was echoed in an interview conducted by Fleet Street journalist Norman Giller. When Clough was appointed as the Rams' new boss, Norman was sent from London to Derby to secure an interview with him. The Derby squad was just about to set off on the team coach when Brian invited Norman on board to ensure he got the article he needed. As the coach made its way to the airport, Norman conducted his interview. 'I remember the wonderful phrase of his was, "I'm going to give Derby a little bit of amnesia and a lot of ambition,"' Norman told me. '"Amnesia – because I don't want anybody talking about the bl***y past. I don't care what Jackie Stamps did. I want to know what my team are going to do next week, not Jackie Stamps 30 years ago. But we're also going to be a club with lots of ambition."' The words 'amnesia and ambition' gave Norman the perfect angle for his story, 'He was going to get rid of your memories of the good days and bring golden days to the Baseball Ground. And he certainly did that.'

Cloughie stayed loyal to Derby even when Coventry came calling with a very attractive offer. He was pictured on the front page of the local newspaper in October 1969 signing a new three-year contract. George Edwards wrote that he understood that Coventry had made Clough a 'massive offer' to succeed Jimmy Hill. The offer would have involved a substantial pay rise. Pictured standing next to Brian as he put pen to paper was Derby chairman Sam Longson. 'I said when Brian Clough came to Derby that the big job would be to keep him here,' said Longson. 'Nothing is more certain than that Brian is going places in football, but I want him to do this with Derby County.' Clough said it was the same contract that had been lying in the club's safe for the past three months. 'It is simply that I have never got round to signing it,' he said. 'Naturally, I was tremendously flattered by the Coventry offer. People like Don Revie and Jock Stein have been mentioned in connection with Coventry and to mention me in the same breath is crazy.'

It was during Derby's promotion season of 1968/69 that Clough produced a classic comment in connection with Middlesbrough. On Boxing Day 1968, Derby had beaten Boro 3-2 at the Baseball Ground. After the match, the Middlesbrough manager Stan Anderson was quoted as saying, 'We are a much better team than

Derby. Take out [Dave] Mackay and [Roy] McFarland and what have you got? Nothing.' When Clough was told about the comment, he replied, 'I know Stan well enough to believe that he said no such thing. He could never be so wrong.' Whack. What a beautifully delivered put-down.

Cloughie was made a Freeman of Derby in 2003, ten years after he had been given the Freedom of Nottingham. When he retired from Forest in 1993, he said he was amazed at how the people of Nottingham had treated him so well over the years. 'I'm absolutely delighted to have been here for 18 years,' he reflected. 'I came here as a boy when I saw my first Test match at Trent Bridge. And I can't believe how good they've been to me.' At the unveiling of his statue in Nottingham, Barbara Clough said the Nottingham people had taken him to their hearts, just as he had taken them to his heart too.

After the European Cup successes, and Peter Taylor had briefly retired then taken over as the Rams' boss, Clough stayed loyal to Forest, despite attempts to lure him back to Derby. He rebuilt the Forest side several times with tremendous success. The annual Wembley trips became part and parcel of supporting the Reds. Reflecting on those later years, in a recorded interview in 2003, he enjoyed referring to the various trophy wins, including the League Cup, 'They were happy days. It's an important competition and it was very near and dear to us. They should have called it the Nottingham Forest Cup, because we were proud to win it. We had a private coach to take us to the finals. We got rid of our driver because the coach knew its own way to Wembley without him.'

Despite the rivalry between Derby and Forest, Cloughie remained proud to have managed both clubs. Not only for what he achieved with them, but for how he did it against the odds. In September 2003, Brian was asked by a Manchester United supporter whether, looking back, he had ever thought about being the manager at Old Trafford. He said that every football boss in the country had thought about it because United were the biggest club in Europe. 'Obviously in your dreams you think about doing it, but I never ever took it seriously in my own mind,' he said. 'I don't think it was a place I was ever destined to go to.' Addressing the fan directly, he added that when his teams had been beating United he sometimes had a yearning to work there. Then came the sucker punch, 'It didn't turn out – and that's the way it goes. I finished up at two big clubs, Derby County and Nottingham Forest.'

14

Clough Exclusive

The label on the cassette includes the listing 'Clough Exclusive'. The tape inside the plastic case has a recording I thought had been lost forever. It's one of my first interviews with Brian Clough. Well, part of it at least.

I managed to grab a few minutes with Cloughie, behind the scenes of a special event in Derby during the early part of his retirement. It was in the days of bulky reel-to-reel tape recorders which you carried by your side thanks to a leather case and shoulder strap.

Throughout the interview it was a case of keeping one eye on the recorder to make sure the tape wasn't snagging in the mechanical recording system and that you weren't about to run out of tape. That's in addition to the much more challenging proposition of facing one of the most unpredictable of interviewees.

It was only a year after the publication of his autobiography in which he admitted that, towards the end of his managerial career, he'd had a drink problem. In fact, he said there were times that alcohol had taken a hold on him and probably affected his professional judgement.

Working as a journalist at the time, I'd been invited to interview him ahead of a personal appearance at Derby Playhouse. Knowing that I needed an angle for a story – and that Brian himself was prepared to talk about it – I took the decision to ask him about the headline-grabbing admission he'd made in his book. Listening back to my recording, it's clear that he didn't duck the controversial subject, even though my heart was in my mouth when I asked the key question after some initial warm-up chit-chat.

'I've read your book – it contains some heart-felt admissions about alcohol – have you beaten the booze?' I asked.

'Totally,' came the reply.

'Tee-total?' I asked firmly.

'Tee-total,' he repeated.

But I didn't leave it there. His responses had been quite short and I was looking for a slightly longer answer.

'And do you think you'll stay that way?'

'Well, I wouldn't like to think I'm going to live for the next 50 years without having one, but if you let me know when I'm going, I'll have one the day before.'

'And are you feeling better for it?'

'Not bad at all thanks. It's been good to see you and I hope to see you again soon, son. Look after yourself.'

Mission accomplished. Cloughie always knew that journalists were looking for an angle to a story. In fact, there were times when he would offer them a 'top line' for an article without the reporter having to probe too much for a headline-grabbing opinion or a new development.

The former journalist Mike Carey, who sadly passed away in 2023, told me a funny story which happened when he was a ghostwriter for Cloughie's regular newspaper column, 'I'll never forget the morning when he burst into his office and said enthusiastically, "I've got today's intro – what a week it's been for saying 'bu**er me'."'

I'm not entirely sure the start of that article would have made it past the subeditors, even though it was Cloughie in his pomp. Mike, who was an experienced writer, was full of great memories like that and there's more about him towards the end of this book.

Back to my visit to Derby Playhouse and Cloughie's special appearance. It was billed as 'An Evening With Brian Clough' and was hosted by the actor Kevin Lloyd, who starred as detective Tosh Lines in the TV drama *The Bill*. I got to know Kevin during my time working in Derby and was delighted when he agreed to be a guest on my BBC radio chat show, *In My Life*, in which he picked some of his favourite music, talked about his life and we visited one of his favourite childhood haunts as part of the programme. On this particular evening at the Playhouse, he was in his element: he was a big Derby County fan and a massive admirer of Brian Clough.

'It's a huge honour to be here and share a stage with the great Brian Clough,' he told me. 'Brian really is a living legend in my eyes. In fact that term "living legend" and the word "great" apply to him more than anyone else I know.'

Kevin said he was pleased the event had attracted a full house. 'This show actually sold out within an hour and a half of the tickets going on sale, which is quite extraordinary,' he said. 'It took everybody by surprise. I was taken by surprise to such an extent that I was contacted in London about the prospects of getting tickets for other people – and even I couldn't get any tickets, and I'm in the thing! Luckily, I've got some now. But it took everybody by surprise to see the complete, amazing sell-out it's become.'

Before the show began, I was invited to a news conference, along with fellow journalists from the national and local media. Sitting where the audience would gather later that evening, I was just a few seats along from the *Sunday Times* columnist Mihir Bose.

One of my lasting memories was the musical theme of the evening. When a reporter began a question by asking, 'Is it true you've been tempted back into football since retiring?' Cloughie quickly made the most of the journalist's pause after the first three words, and started to give a rendition of the 1930s classic 'Is it true what they say about Dixie?' After singing the opening line, which is the song's title, he continued crooning the lyrics, 'Does the sun really shine all the time? Do the sweet magnolias blossom at everybody's door?'

Apart from the surprise of seeing Cloughie burst into song in front of a group of journalists, what also struck me was the heavy emphasis on the word 'door', sung in the American-style of the 'King of Cool' Dean Martin, who recorded a version of the song in the 1950s. In a knock-about and comical exchange with a journalist towards the end of the aborted sing-song, the reporter shouted 'Get off!' – to which Brian responded with a roar of laughter, before answering the question.

He admitted he had been approached by Derby County and Notts County to return to football, but had declined both offers. The only position he would consider, he said, was that of a programme seller on matchdays.

The music of the Rat Pack continued into the show that evening. Following Kevin Lloyd's introduction of Clough as 'a living legend', he walked on to the stage to the accompaniment of Frank Sinatra's 'My Way'. The show closed with Brian leading a rendition of Sinatra's 'Come Fly With Me' before the audience got to its feet to show its appreciation (although not necessarily of the singing!) with a standing ovation.

Listening to some of the recordings I've collected, Cloughie's love of a good old sing-song is definitely a consistent theme, even when the media was around. Perhaps it was their presence that spurred him on. During a 106 Century FM phone-in, he waxed lyrical – much to the embarrassment of his young grandson Stephen, who was with him in the studio.

The topic under discussion that evening was the rigours of football management and how Cloughie felt it was important to 'learn your trade' at the bottom of the ladder, such as in non-league football. His former striker Garry Birtles was also in the studio and admitted how difficult he had found it having taken charge of Gresley Rovers from 1997 to 1999. 'It was hard work … I wouldn't go back to it,' said Birtles. 'I think you need to be a special kind of person to be able to do that week-in, week-out.' At that point, Birtles paused and realised he had repeated a football cliché he had vowed not to repeat: week-in, week-out. 'We've banned it on this programme,' joked host Darren Fletcher, 'and the only one who says it is Garry.' That was Brian's cue. 'There's a song called "Week In, Week Out",' he said. 'Sinatra sings it.' And you can guess what happened next. Correct. The famous Sinatra fan started to croon. 'Don't sing, Grandad,' said young Stephen, to which Brian replied, 'Don't sing, no, it's one of my strong points, singing. And if you believe that, you believe anything.'

* * *

Another interview I found in the box of recordings was my conversation with Brian at a book shop when his first autobiography was launched. I was working for the BBC at the original Broadcasting House in London when I received the invitation to interview Cloughie, not far from where he lived in Derby. At that stage, he had rarely conducted any radio interviews since his retirement around 18 months earlier.

It was a live interview, so you can imagine the nerves were jangling at the thought of things possibly not going to plan. Face-to-face with my footballing hero, I was so nervous that I started the interview by getting the time of day wrong, 'I'm with a living legend where football is concerned – the former Derby County and Nottingham Forest manager Brian Clough, who's here signing copies of his autobiography. Good morning, Mr Clough, or should I say good afternoon?' (I quickly realised that while waiting for the presenter to introduce me, we'd now gone past midday).

'Marcus, good afternoon to you too, although it's not a very good afternoon, it's pouring down outside. But it's nice to see you.'

'Yes, it's a bit wet, isn't it?' I said, having got absolutely soaked during the walk from the radio studio to the nearby Clulow's bookshop, carrying the heavy broadcasting device over my shoulder.

Listening back to the recording, the signal from my mobile broadcasting unit started to break up (we were in the back room of the book shop) and there was a sharp crackling sound which distorted part of my first question. Luckily that technical problem didn't last long and the interview continued, even though I was completely unaware the listeners had heard this interference.

'It's nearly 18 months since you retired, how is the life of leisure suiting you?'

'Absolutely magnificently,' came the reply. 'I'm enjoying every second. I think I should have done it five years ago. It's a wonderful feeling to get up of a morning, knowing you can just please yourself and do what you want to do. I've found my life so full, it's incredible. I like Derbyshire, obviously, I've been here 27 years. It's just living what people call a normal life, but it's not "normal" as such, or humdrum, it's a beautiful time.

'I've got my grandchildren, I've got holidays, I've got a garden, I've got lanes to walk down. I've got your lovely smiling face to look at on a Saturday – God forbid!'

And yes, I *was* smiling! I felt buoyed by the fact he was in the mood for a good chat and it turned into a wonderful, entertaining interview.

'What do you do on a Saturday, now you haven't got a match?' I asked.

'Well, sometimes I sit and watch the rugby, I'm very interested in rugby. I'm looking forward to the cricket starting. Then I get out and about and do everything that everybody else does. I'm planning to start to go and see a few matches in the new year, because I've avoided going to football matches since I retired. I've been to a couple to see my son play in the Liverpool reserves, but apart from that I've stayed clear all together. But I think I'll pick the threads up after Christmas and into the new year.'

On another occasion, Brian was keen to make the point that Nigel deserved a first-team place. 'I'm not saying it because I'm biased,' he told me and a group of other journalists. 'He's got enough talent to be playing on somebody's football ground every single week. Now, whether it be Doncaster Rovers or whether it be Liverpool, he's got the talent to get into somebody's first team. I think it's a terrible waste that he's not actually involved.'

Nigel had been signed by Liverpool boss Graeme Souness in 1993 and began his Anfield career with a blistering debut against Trevor Francis's Sheffield Wednesday, putting two goals past former Nottingham Forest goalkeeper Chris Woods in a 2-0 win. After the match, Liverpool defender and fellow new boy Neil Ruddock said of Nigel, 'Playing against him, he has always been a tough opponent, so having him in our side is a great bonus. I think Brian Clough will be happy with his young man.' Nigel scored again four days later in a 3-1 victory at Queens Park Rangers. Despite his enormous talent, he later enjoyed fewer starts at Anfield, especially when Souness was replaced by Roy Evans. As his father said, it was indeed a terrible waste at that time. When *The Guardian* reported Liverpool's amazing comeback from being 3-0 down at home to a Manchester United side that included Nigel's former Forest team-mate Roy Keane, the article described

Clough as the key figure in midfield in the first 45 minutes. He scored twice in a scintillating match which ended 3-3. The article continued, 'On this night he seemed transformed. "You have seen the best of me but not enough of me," he told Liverpool supporters recently. They had not. Clough has rarely played better and was to crown his performance with Liverpool's first two goals.'

Alex Ferguson was said to have been left stunned by losing a 3-0 lead. Nigel's dad would have enjoyed that too!

* * *

In my 'bookshop interview' with Cloughie, he was particularly outspoken about one of his favourite subjects – the job security (or lack of it) of football managers. There had been a spate of managerial sackings and I asked him what he thought about the situation.

'It's been a mad month for top-class managers and top class clubs,' he said. 'I don't know what's going on in the minds of chairmen and directors at the moment, but they're not coming up with remedies, they're just a short-term answer and it's reached epidemic proportions.

'If they really want to show they're sincere, then by all means sack the managers – but they should resign as chairmen too, because initially it's their decision to appoint them.'

He told me that the fear of getting the sack should be removed from the thoughts of managers altogether, 'The game's hard enough without having this in the background every time you get out of bed each morning.'

* * *

I was fortunate to record another interview with Brian nearly ten years later. It was one of those occasions when you hoped he would be on good form, but he still liked to keep you on your toes. The afternoon started well as he signed copies of the updated edition of his autobiography in WHSmith in Nottingham's Victoria Centre. The queue of admirers eager to meet him spilled out of the main entrance of the store. As Cloughie sat at a table signing books and other memorabilia, I was standing a few feet away, taking photographs for my tribute website. Suddenly, he stopped signing the books for the long queue of fans and looked up in my direction.

For a moment, I knew exactly what John Robertson meant when he recalled how Cloughie had what he described as an 'elephant's brain' – his memory was amazing. The simplest thing, insignificant to most other people, would be stored away in his head, ready to be used to great effect when you least expected it.

Wagging that famous finger, he pointed towards me and, slightly raising his voice, asked, 'Are you the young man who brought that pile of messages for me?' Like a frightened rabbit caught in the headlights of a car, I was frozen to the spot, in front of dozens of customers waiting to have their books signed.

Let me explain the background to this. A few months earlier, I had visited Brian's house, unannounced, to deliver a pile of 'get well' messages that I had received via the tribute website's email address. Barbara answered the door and thanked me for taking the time to print them all out and deliver them personally. Yet now, here I was, wondering whether I was about to get a rollicking for turning up at his house unannounced. It was obvious he had recognised me, so honesty seemed the best policy. 'Yes, Mr Clough, it was me,' I replied.

He then got out of his chair, leant forward and put his arm out to shake my hand. 'Thanks very much for all those messages you delivered, young man,' he said. 'It was very much appreciated.'

He then suggested we should have a chat – which we did when the signing session was over. The recording still makes me laugh, for reasons which will become clear shortly. I told him he was looking well. 'Young man, thank you. I'm in good nick,' he said. I asked him how important the support of Barbara had been. 'It's been incredible,' he replied – and with tongue firmly in cheek he added, 'I thought about changing her for a younger model a few years ago, but she's stuck it for 44 years, so it's been fine.'

He described how Barbara had taken a phone call one Sunday night to tell them that a liver was available for his transplant and it was on its way from Ireland. They then made the trip to the hospital in the north-east. I asked him if he could remember his first request for something to eat after the operation. I knew it was a question which promised a humorous answer. But I didn't quite expect just how comical he would be – and how relieved I was that the interview wasn't live.

He told me he had asked the hospital staff for an apple sandwich, 'I quite like apple sandwiches – the only thing is, they don't keep apples in hospitals.' I then started to wonder where the story was going. He described how the nurse was short-sighted and he feared he might lose certain parts of his anatomy. 'It's not live, is it?' asked Cloughie, looking at the microphone I was holding. 'Thankfully not,' I replied, just about keeping my laughter in check. 'Ah, that's all right. You won't last another six months in this job if you follow me around.'

From memory, Archie Gemmill and Ron Fenton were also in the room and were chuckling in the background. Thankfully, the great quotes didn't end there. While describing his surgeon, Derek Manas, as 'incredible' he delivered the type of praise that could only come from Old Big 'Ead, 'He's supposed to be in the top three in the country, but he told me he was the best. Conceited – it's incredible. I said to him, "They'll have to widen the hospital doors if you and I walk in together, because they'd never get both heads through one door, would they?"'

Our conversation lasted for about 15 minutes and, as you might expect, I didn't escape being on the receiving end of a classic one-liner. As he praised the whole NHS team at Newcastle's Freeman Hospital, he added, 'I thanked them then – and I'm thanking them again now. It's an incredible situation and an incredible experience. But I'm in good nick. I want to take you around with me for the next three, four or five weeks, because you definitely make me better-looking than I am – and it's understandable obviously!'

* * *

One of the videos I found in the box of Cloughie memories was footage of my meeting with him in 2002, including some BBC pictures. Thanks to a video player (remember those?) borrowed from my father-in-law Roland, it was a superb 'step back in time' to watch the main man in top form in front of a crowd of fans. The occasion was another book signing. He had agreed to sign copies of *Walking on Water* at the Asda supermarket in West Bridgford, not far from the City Ground. It was the first signing session he did for the book, even though the official publication date was several days later.

The publishers had said he would personally sign copies for the first 300 people. I was so determined that I arrived more than five hours before he was due to appear. And I was not alone. My girlfriend (now wife) Sarah was with me too. Luckily for me, Sarah is almost as big a fan of Cloughie as I am. So, there we were, standing outside Asda at quarter to six in the morning. We arrived so early that we were the first in the queue.

Watching the grainy footage, there was no mistaking the spontaneous applause when he appeared from a side door and the crowd began singing his name. It still sent a shiver down my back all these years later. It was captivating to see him stand there with a big grin on his face, soaking up the adulation. He blew a kiss and shouted above the singing, 'Good morning to you!'

Sarah and I were both nervously waiting to be introduced to him. 'Where's Sarah? I've been told I've got to meet Sarah,' said Cloughie as he started to make his way through the crowd. An assistant from the publishing company realised it was going to be a difficult task for him to make his way through the mass of people, so she guided him towards us. 'Sarah's over here, at the front of the queue,' she told him.

He walked towards us and, with a big smile, shook Sarah's hand and then mine. Leaning forward, I said, 'It's great to meet you, Mr Clough.'

'Nice to meet you, too, young man,' he replied, before asking where we lived. When Sarah said she came from Gedling in Nottingham, his eyes lit up. 'That's a pit area, isn't it? I've got a statue from Gedling Pit. They gave it to me.' His support for the miners during the 1984 strike is well remembered to this day.

Cloughie then presented us with a bottle of champagne for being the first in the queue. It was a bottle of Moët & Chandon – the significance of which was not lost on him. In the books he was signing that day, he admitted that drink had caused an adverse effect on his health and there were times it had impaired his judgement. So, as he handed over the bottle, he joked, 'You're trying to get me on the booze again, aren't you?'

A newspaper photographer, who knew Cloughie well, asked us to pose for a photo. Trevor Bartlett from the *Nottingham Evening Post* had worked with Brian for many years and he captured some great pictures that day. As the three of us stood close together, Cloughie looked at me, smiled and joked to Trevor, 'Hurry up, I've heard he's famous for getting people's wallets.' There was more laughter.

Then Brian gave Sarah a kiss. It was a special moment and one I know Sarah will never forget. In fact, he kissed her on the cheek twice, at Trevor's request – to ensure he got the photo he wanted. 'Thank you, Mr Clough,' said Sarah, being careful not to drop the champagne bottle. Cloughie pointed to the bubbly. 'It goes well in the bath,' he told us. 'We used to bathe in that. It's easy when you win to have a glass of champagne. And the excuse when I lost was I thought I'd drown my bloomin' sorrows.'

'But that didn't happen very often – you didn't lose many, Mr Clough,' Sarah replied, as he sat down to start signing our books. 'That's right,' he replied. 'I had a good run, pet, I had a good run.'

Despite the long queue of fans, Brian lavished his time on us. In an interview with Brian Moore many years ago, he said he and Barbara had brought their children up to be generous with their time and generous with their smiles. He was certainly abiding by that principle himself as we chatted to him. Then came some advice, 'If you get chance, go and see a good side play – Burton Albion.' We were able to say we had already seen the Brewers in action several times at Eton Park, where Nigel had become manager in 1998. Cloughie had a reserved seat there and we would always make a special effort to look out for him. 'It costs me a fortune at half-time for my grandchildren, with all the chips and burgers,' he told us. 'You'd think they never got fed at home!'

And that reminds me. The Burton Albion fanzine at the time, called *Clough the Magic Dragon*, once secured an exclusive interview with their famous fan. Burton had just beaten Chester 2-0 and Brian said the result had given him a boost. 'It makes my week when Burton do well, especially to keep a clean sheet,' he added. He admitted it was unfortunate that Albion had lost quite a few home matches. Then he delivered the perfect punchline, 'I was actually hoping that Burton would lose today, because I was going to put in for the job if they sacked the manager.' Brilliant.

15

Post a Letter

More than 20 years after being turned down for the job of England manager, the decision still rankled with Cloughie. If any evidence of this was required, you only had to listen to his powerful and passionate response when he was asked about the decision at a football forum. His reply took no prisoners. Yes, he was playing to the crowd, who responded in support as his voice grew louder. But nobody was left in any doubt about how strongly he still felt all those years later.

The recording of the forum was broadcast on regional commercial radio a few days after the Pride Park Stadium event. The evening witnessed possibly his strongest attack on the FA officials who failed to appoint him as England boss.

'I got the feeling that Lancaster Gate were frightened of me,' he said. 'That's because I'd have been a little more open and I'd have asked, possibly, what qualifications they had to be with the FA. Somebody might have stood up and said I've been a postman for 30 years.' At this point the audience began laughing. 'And I would have said, "Go and post a ***** letter then!"' The laughter grew even louder.

He went on to explain how confident he had felt about securing the job as he'd left the FA headquarters. 'We all know when we do good things,' he said. 'I came out of the interview and I'd got a couple of friends in the hotel opposite at Lancaster Gate and they asked me how it had gone. I said that, as interviews go, I've walked it. And I had – I'd captured them. Their mouths were open.'

Clough told the audience that he had the necessary experience for the job, both as a player and a manager. 'And then of course, I didn't get it.' The only comfort, he said, was that neither Jack Charlton nor Lawrie McMenemy got it either, 'True to the Football Association, they went for the easy way out and appointed Ron Greenwood. And he wasn't even on the shortlist.'

Brian said the officials had chosen Greenwood because he was a charming man and 'wouldn't say boo to a goose'. He added that the FA knew they would get excited watching Greenwood's teams 'because he couldn't keep a clean sheet to save his bl**dy life with West Ham'.

It was at this point that Brian's voice began to gradually get louder, as the injustice he still felt spilt out with full force, 'He [Greenwood] fitted the bill. *Their* bill. They weren't worried about *you*. They weren't worried about the standing of English football throughout Europe. They weren't worried about gates. They were worried about *themselves*. They didn't want me invading.'

Clough suggested the FA's decision was due to some people in the football hierarchy being jealous of what he had achieved. He admitted that, at the time of the interview, he hadn't appreciated that some people would be jealous of his success – even though he hadn't won the league title for a second time at that point. He told the audience that his assistant Peter Taylor had told him that even some fellow managers, who had been in the game for longer, would not be happy with him because he had achieved greater success in a shorter period of time.

In his autobiography, Clough said he thought he had 'cracked it' once the interview was over. He'd gone into Lancaster Gate full of confidence as 'the people's choice'. However, he wasn't the choice of Nottingham Forest fans who wanted him to stay at the City Ground. A local campaign was launched by the *Nottingham Evening Post* to keep him at Forest. Clough challenged fans to prove to him that they wanted him to stay. He asked them to buy season tickets – and in response the cash rolled into the City Ground. One newspaper reported, 'Nottingham Forest fans have launched a spending spree in a desperate bid to keep manager Brian Clough.'

Supporters queued up to buy season tickets, even though it was mid-season, with 200 being sold over a couple of days. Forest secretary Ken Smales said, 'Everybody taking a ticket has made it clear they don't want to lose Brian.' Mr Smales added that the club had banked an extra £6,000 which was remarkable for that stage of the season. That figure was increased to £10,000 after three days. There were crowds outside the stadium when Clough arrived for work at the City Ground on Friday, 11 November 1977.

One newspaper had the headline 'Fan-Tastic!' alongside a photograph of Brian standing alongside his famous sign declaring 'Gentlemen, No Swearing Please! Brian' which had been shown to the City Ground's Trent End before the previous home match against Middlesbrough. Speaking about the response of the fans – following a previous statement that support for Forest could persuade him to abandon interest in the England job – Brian commented, 'I have never seen queues like them in November. Tomorrow we are playing Manchester United, the biggest club in Europe. But I bet they haven't sold as many season tickets this week as we have. Frankly, I'm surprised. I have never doubted the Forest fans were behind me. I just didn't feel there were enough of them.'

Yet *The Sun* campaigned for him to be England boss, including pin badges declaring 'Clough for England' (I've still got one of them). The *Daily Mirror* produced a special poll of football's big names and published the results under the headline 'Clough Justice!'. Its 12-man jury, said the *Mirror*, had delivered a verdict 'which nearly every soccer fan hopes will become fact'. This expert panel, including football legends such as Bill Shankly, Sir Tom Finney and Jock Stein, had been asked to consider four names for England's top job: Lawrie McMenemy of Southampton, Sir Bobby Robson of Ipswich, the interim boss Ron Greenwood and Brian Clough.

'It must be Brian Clough,' declared former England forward Sir Tom, who played in four World Cups. 'He's the man with the Midas touch, the man who can motivate ordinary players into great ones. He's the man to restore what's missing at international level – pride. He can make our players believe in themselves again, make them great. We certainly need him now before it's too late.'

However, World Cup winner Martin Peters was among the nay-sayers, although he admitted he was probably influenced to vote for Greenwood because of his West Ham background. 'It is very difficult to give an opinion on people I don't know – and I don't know the methods of Clough, Robson or McMenemy,' said Peters. 'But I do know Ron Greenwood and I would think given time and opportunity he would do a good job. There again, I was brought up the West Ham way and played to his style.'

The *Mirror* 'jury' also included the Leeds United and England player Allan Clarke. He said he had tremendous respect for Sir Bobby, having played with him at Fulham. 'But I have to be realistic and say that Clough has the edge. He's won things,' he added. Shankly described the contest as 'a one-horse race', with Clough being the only name worthy of the top job. 'He converted Derby from a pig-sty to a league championship club,' said Shanks. 'He has taken Nottingham Forest, a pigeon loft from the Second Division, to the top of the First. He is an optimist and he's a winner.' Duncan McKenzie, who had played for Brian at Leeds, also chose his former boss. However, the former Scotland manager Jock Stein pointed out that being a successful club boss didn't automatically translate into success in the national job. He said that while Clough was obviously a great motivator, 'The most successful club motivator was given the job the last time and everyone hailed Don Revie as the perfect appointment.' After initial success, Revie's tenure had ultimately ended in disappointment along with his controversial departure to the United Arab Emirates. Nevertheless, Clough remained the overwhelming choice of this panel of experts, with former Manchester United and Scotland player Denis Law summing up the common viewpoint, 'English football needs a lift at this particular time. It needs character ... it needs Brian Clough.'

In the *Liverpool Echo*, the tough-tackling defender Tommy Smith used his newspaper column to champion Cloughie for the England job, 'Clough would generate more enthusiasm overnight than has been worked up over England for years.' Bearing in mind that England had failed to qualify for the 1978 World Cup, that view was quite understandable. In fact, Smith went further and said Clough should have been made England manager in 1974 rather than Revie. 'He [Clough] can add that little bit of fire that has been missing, and there's no doubt he would gain the respect of the players,' added Smith. He said the players that Brian had worked with 'think the world of him', although I'm not convinced that was entirely true during his 44 days at Leeds.

* * *

Just a few days after being turned down for the England job, Clough was interviewed by a national newspaper about the decision, which he admitted 'hit me hard'. However, he went on to say that he tried to keep his emotions under control, 'I bit my tongue and kept my head. I did not plunge head-long into the River Trent.' Well, at least that was showing some restraint! Seriously though, he said the seven-man committee hadn't consisted of the 'ogres' he'd expected, 'For more than one hour we talked about the state of English football and I felt so comfortable that I could have stayed on for a further 24 hours.' Clough said he had even raised a laugh at the end of the interview when he addressed the chairman, Sir Harold Thompson, as being not as bad a guy as he and his fellow managers had thought he was. Brian said there had been no hostility in the room and the atmosphere had been a good one.

Cloughie also said he still didn't know why he didn't get the job, 'I had qualifications like success wherever I've been, my coaching badges and 12 years of managerial experience. I had a very good interview, it was a wonderful experience before a formidable set of administrators.' That response made me smile a little because I remember listening to Brian talk at a fundraising dinner in Stoke, long after he had retired. During the evening, in May 2001, he spoke about being turned down for the England job – and his comments about the panel of officials who had interviewed him were not quite so glowing. He was playing to the audience at the time as he declared, 'There were ten of them on the interview panel. And four of them had been dead for a year. What's more, the other six hadn't twigged.'

Coming back to the newspaper interview following his rejection, Cloughie added that he had thanked the FA secretary, Ted Croker, for telling him the decision personally, despite a journalist informing him beforehand. 'That is the way of the football world,' reflected Brian. And he became even more philosophical about the decision when he said that his family had become of 'prime importance' when he arrived home at 11 o'clock that night. 'If you really want to know, I sensed a feeling of relief rather than disappointment,' he continued. 'And I didn't have to remind myself that I was the manager of a team at the top of the First Division.' It was a great comfort, he said, that a petition with more than 4,000 signatures was on his office desk. It was signed by Nottingham Forest supporters asking him not to leave. A newspaper report quoted the petition organiser, Derek Page, who said that Reds fans dreaded the idea of Clough becoming England boss, 'He has said the fans could influence him and we hope our petition will show that there is the support at the City Ground to carry the club right to the top.'

* * *

Although Brian told the *Sunday Mirror*'s Vince Wilson in 1977 that he didn't know why he didn't get the England job, it's a good bet that his outspoken nature counted against him. The former Fleet Street journalist Norman Giller told me that Cloughie would have stood a better chance of securing the nation's top footballing post if he had been able to utilise 'an internal filter.' Norman explained more in my *Green Jumper* podcast, 'Brian was his own worst enemy. He was so outspoken. He needed to have had some sort of internal mechanism that could have stopped him talking. If he could have held back some of his opinions he wouldn't have frightened the top brass. But Brian loved to let people know exactly what he felt and sometimes that hurt people's feelings.'

Yet if Cloughie had censored himself on certain subjects, it wouldn't have been the same Cloughie that fans knew and loved to hear about. In a BBC interview during his retirement, he reflected on whether he could have done things differently during his career. 'I could have been a little bit less aggressive, but then that would have taken away something from what I had,' he said.

Shortly after being appointed Nottingham Forest manager in January 1975, he pledged to avoid making outspoken comments which could spark unwanted controversy. A newspaper headline declared 'Shut That Mouth – I'll be trying so hard, says Brian Clough'. The first two sentences of his newspaper column read like this, 'I promise to keep my mouth shut and never invite trouble. That's the pledge I have taken with my wife Barbara – my new year resolution on my return to football.'

He went on to explain that while his passion for football and 'unquenchable thirst' for success would never change, his image may become 'less explosive'. It was probably a case of wishful thinking. I feel it was that passion for the game – and the desire to win matches in the right way – that drove him to be outspoken about aspects of the game he disagreed with. It was always going to be virtually impossible for him to change his image, as he hinted in the column's third paragraph, 'Sadly, I fear, all resolutions are broken, but I swear I'll be trying.' The footballing public generally loved Cloughie as he was – even if the footballing authorities had the opposite view.

Norman Giller was spot-on when he said the FA were frightened of Clough because they thought he would run every aspect of English football, 'And too right, he would have done! He would have sorted the FA out. Brian had this great idea of tackling football from the grassroots, to get the kids involved. He was going to change the FA from top to bottom and his main idea was to bring through the youth of the country.'

There's no doubt that one of Cloughie's great passions was working with young players and seeing them progress. Perhaps it's something that went back to his first introduction into management as coach of the youth team at Sunderland. Many years later, in a preview for an FA Youth Cup semi-final against Arsenal, he described how rewarding it was to see youngsters arrive at Nottingham Forest, straight from school, and go on to make the grade. 'It's like watching little crocuses grow,' he said. 'I would love to do nothing else for two or three months than see a shoot come out of the ground, develop into a bud and see it blossom into a lovely, colourful flower. Seeing our kids develop is the nearest I'll get to it because sadly I don't have the time to sit and watch my garden grow.'

He went on to say it was a pleasure to work with the young players, who went about their work with a smile, 'They cheer me up some mornings when I'm not at my best and to see their fresh young faces is one of the reasons why I keep coming into work. As long as they keep smiling, I'll postpone my retirement to watch the crocuses grow for a little while longer.' Forest's youth team squad at the time included Steve Stone, Gary Charles and Lee Glover.

Talking of Steve Stone, I found an archive interview in which Cloughie expressed his regret at not playing the midfielder more often during his final season, when Forest were relegated. The interview, part of my collection of tape cassettes, was recorded in October 2003 and Brian was speaking ahead of Forest's match against Portsmouth, where Stone was then playing.

The young Geordie had suffered badly with injuries during his time at the City Ground, including breaking a leg several times. After scoring the winner in his full senior debut (a header in a 2-1 win at Middlesbrough in February 1993), Stone began to secure more regular first-team starts. 'I was used to putting him in ambulances with broken legs and that type of thing,' said Clough, before admitting, 'I underestimated the young man. I should have played him a little bit more in the first team ... but I was obsessed with a lad called Gary Crosby. Steve has blossomed much to my delight. I'm absolutely delighted for him. He's had a rough ride and he's now had a little bit of success with Portsmouth – and he's played for England, hasn't he? How many caps did he get?' The reporter, Nick Wilson, said he thought it was nine caps. 'I only got two, son,' replied Brian. 'And I *could* play, you can't.'

If you look at some of the other young players Clough introduced into the game, such as Roy McFarland, Roy Keane and his own son, Nigel (to name just a few), his record for unearthing fresh talent is quite staggering. 'You pick your best side – and age doesn't come into it,' he once told a radio programme. 'If they're good enough, they're old enough.' And he clearly appreciated how overwhelming it could be for a young player to appear in football's top flight. That's why he told Keane about his debut at Anfield just minutes before the match was due to start. There was no time to get anxious and tense.

In an archive recording I found on one of my cassettes, Clough talked about bringing young players into the professional game, 'When my son made his debut, I said to him, "What was the one thing that hit you more than anything else?" You know what he said? It took me by surprise. He said, "The noise. [I was] playing in the reserves in front of two or three thousand and suddenly I was in front of around 20,000 and the noise nearly knocked my head off." Now, I wouldn't have thought that because, hell, I got 31,000 in my testimonial match, let alone the few thousand that used to go down to the City Ground. So, it does take different things to get to different players. Young players have got to learn all the tricks of the trade.' And getting used to the impact of a huge crowd was just one of those aspects of the game. In some ways, the way Gareth Southgate has utilised England's young talent is an indication of what Clough may also have striven to achieve. I'm confident that, given the chance, the World Cup would have returned to England with Clough in charge.

When England were beaten 2-1 by Norway in Oslo in 1981, the calls for Clough to be the national boss grew louder. The match is often remembered for the radio commentary of the Norwegian broadcaster Bjørge Lillelien. In 1981, the Norwegians were not considered to be a major footballing nation. They had not qualified for the World Cup finals since 1938 and some of their squad were still part-timers. The England team included the likes of Kevin Keegan, Bryan Robson, Glenn Hoddle, Trevor Francis and goalkeeper Ray Clemence. It's impossible to think that Clough would not have got the very best out of this group of players. Yet, despite taking the lead with a Robson goal, they lost the match – to the delight of Lillelian, whose joyful prose entered football folklore, 'Lord Nelson, Lord Beaverbrook, Sir Winston Churchill, Sir Anthony Eden, Clement Attlee, Henry Cooper, Lady Diana, we have beaten them all!'

This was followed by a famous call to the British prime minister, 'Maggie Thatcher, can you hear me? I have a message for you. Norway have knocked England out of the World Cup. As they say in your language in the boxing bars around Madison Square Garden in New York, your boys took a helluva beating. Your boys took a helluva beating!'

Yes, it was quite a beating, but England *did* qualify for the 1982 World Cup. Nevertheless, just days after the defeat by Norway, the clamour for Clough to be brought in to 'save' England reached fever pitch. One national newspaper conducted a poll of supporters and declared, 'Come in Brian Clough – your country needs you!' The article reminded readers that England had failed to qualify for the finals since Chile in 1962. In 1966 England had qualified as hosts, while in 1970 they were in Mexico as defending champions. But in 1974 in West Germany, and 1978 in Argentina, they were absent. Mindful of Brian's tendency to be outspoken, the newspaper asked the question, 'But why go for Cloughie – the man acknowledged as the most controversial manager of our time? The message is simple. To revive an ailing England soccer side sliding from disaster to disaster.'

And they didn't stop there. The situation was described as 'nothing short of a national disgrace' while Clough was hailed as 'the messiah to lead England back to soccer greatness'.

Even a leading advocate for Ron Greenwood back in 1977 changed his mind and gave his full backing to Clough. In the *Sunday Mirror*'s 12-man 'jury' four years previously, the then Norwich manager John Bond said, 'So far as I am concerned the question is academic … there is only one candidate and he's Ron Greenwood. His tactical knowhow at international level is so superior to that of all the other names being bandied around that it amazes me there is any doubt at all.' But following the result in Oslo, Bond – who by then had become the Manchester City boss – said Clough was the natural successor to Greenwood. 'The people at the highest level of the game have got to be seen to make the right decision on this,' he said. 'They can't fiddle about with it, even if that means making a decision that they might not be 100 per cent behind themselves. Even if they don't fancy Clough, but feel he is the man for the job, they should still give it him. I think he's the only man for England.'

A newspaper poll of thousands of football supporters gave Clough 34 per cent of the vote, with Greenwood on 24 per cent and Sir Bobby Robson on 17 per cent. After Sir Bobby succeeded Greenwood in 1982, the calls for Clough to be appointed became so strong that he offered to resign to allow Brian to take over.

In a 1984 interview with the BBC's excellent sports correspondent Pat Murphy, who Clough worked closely with over many years, Brian admitted that the chance of him being England manager had, by then, passed him by. He insisted that he had been right for the job in 1977 and that he felt the interview had gone extremely well.

'You always know when you've done something well, if you've got any sense at all,' he said. 'A footballer knows when he plays well. I assume you know when you've done a good programme. And I knew I'd had a good interview – and it was ripe at that time for me to have the job.' Clough said that appointing Sir Bobby was 'the best decision they've made for a long time'. Murphy asked Brian whether he thought the job had now gone for him. 'Oh yes, it's gone, yes,' he replied. He was then asked why he thought he'd missed out. 'I think they were a little bit wary of me,' he said. 'I didn't think I knew them as well as possibly they would have liked to have known me, because I'm not one to be hob-knobbing in boardrooms. And I think they might have had a sneaking suspicion that I would have run the English Football Association – and I certainly would have done.'

If an interview with the BBC's David Coleman more than a decade earlier was anything to go by, the 'sneaking suspicion' that Clough referred to was more likely to have been a firm fear. The recording has since become an iconic Clough interview and an excerpt of it is often repeated when any programme looks back on his life. 'I would like the supreme job of dictating football,' he said. 'And I mean dictating football right down to the school level and right down to the coaching level.' He would set out a blueprint for how the game should be run and played, 'I'd be so hard on some people, it would be unbelievable. There would be no millionaire pools people while there are struggling football clubs. I'd put that right overnight ... dictators are out, but I would love to be the perfect dictator.'

When Cloughie's retirement was announced in 1993, the *Daily Mirror* didn't hide its anger over the FA's previous failures to appoint him to the top job. The headline declared 'Clough: He should have been the manager of England'.

A passionate article by the *Mirror*'s sports editor, Keith Fisher, referred to the 'Colonel Blimps' of Lancaster Gate who should 'hang their heads in shame'. Alongside a photo of Cloughie giving his famous 'thumbs-up', Fisher said that you only had to look at the men who had held the job instead to see what England had missed out on. He said Ron Greenwood 'was all about confusing blackboard tactics' and Sir Bobby Robson was 'the man who could never make up his mind'. Meanwhile, Fisher said the real destiny for Graham Taylor – who had taken over from Sir Bobby in 1990 – 'was Watford Football Club and the long ball game'. Perhaps that was a little harsh on the men in question. After all, the England job has become something of a poisoned chalice over the years. Nevertheless, Fisher was correct when he said that England would have benefitted from 'the genius of a man who could make players play'.

Behind the scenes, the odds had always been stacked heavily against Clough getting the top job. This was made crystal clear in an ITV documentary which was later turned into a popular DVD. The programme shed light on the sham surrounding the interview process in 1977. Former FA press officer Glen Kirton told the programme, 'The decision had already been made that Ron Greenwood was the preferred candidate. There wasn't a vote. Sir Harold Thompson would have said, "I want to appoint Ron Greenwood," and they would have agreed. The decision was made beforehand. Ron Greenwood was not on the candidate list.' Kirton's comments represented the first time anybody from the FA had broken ranks and admitted that one man, Thompson, was responsible for shaping the destiny of English football. 'It would have been his absolute dream job,' said Barbara Clough in the programme.

Although the dream was never to become reality, the *Mirror*'s Keith Fisher summed it up well when he concluded, 'The great British public must always remember Brian Clough as the advocate of a beautiful, simple game that has been complicated over the years by fools.'

16

Clough's Football Philosophy

In a 2004 magazine article, Cloughie was asked to explain his managerial philosophy. 'Put it in a book and it'll replace the Bible in every hotel room in the country,' he replied. He then described it as 'one-tenth ability and nine-tenths common sense'. Getting into his stride, his answer continued with the self-assurance of someone who was still very much 'on the ball'.

'Conceit goes with talent – sorting out the club, your background staff and spotting those who can play – and I'm entitled to be conceited. Many people who have interviewed me down the years were astonished that I knew the answers before they'd finished their questions. Not my fault if they weren't all that good at their jobs.'

The late Mike Carey used to write Brian's twice-weekly column for a national newspaper when he was Derby manager. Mike recalled, 'Between times, he would discuss his plans for the future. "Eventually we will have a team here so good that even you could manage it," he would say. "Every year we will go out and buy just one player – but he will be the best player in the country."'

Mike described it as a privilege to work with Cloughie, 'Most of the time, it was a question of what to leave out of his column, not what to put in (unlike the case of another well-known manager who expected his ghostwriter to have his column written before they met up each week).'

I often think about how great it would be to hear Brian's opinions on the football issues of today. Mike agreed, 'He would have had much to say about football agents, about managers who criticise referees or who can't control their players ... and, young man, it would have all made sense.'

The various recordings I collected over the years included one from 2001, in which Cloughie looked back at some of the qualities which brought success. It was a joy to listen to him talk with pride when he described his footballing style. It's a principle which stands the test of time, 'I ensured we played football the way it should be played, which was on the grass. Now, if God had wanted us to play in the clouds, he'd have put a pitch up there. There are far too many managers who came in the game and took the easy way out and started booting the ball 50, 60, or 70 yards and drove everybody crackers. We came to the top playing football, irrespective of whether we were losing, winning or drawing. We kept the ball and played it. We adapted to the conditions and built an understanding between us.'

A beautifully written report in Dublin's *Sunday Independent* in December 1989 described exactly how Clough's teams were the perfect illustration of the beautiful game in all its glory. Outlining how Forest had quickly turned around a 1-0 deficit at Spurs to lead 2-1, including a goal from Nigel, and won 3-2, the article stated, 'Brian Clough's 1,000th game as a Football League manager became a celebration inside half an hour. Toasted with some of the game's best values ... speed, skill and a willingness to move the ball from man to man in that sweet old-fashioned away.'

There was no wonder that the *Independent*'s report also described how Brian repeatedly leapt to his feet with excitement during the match. Forest went 3-1 up and Gary Lineker's second goal was said to carry 'only cosmetic value ... this was Brian Clough's day, at times a spectacular underlining of his contribution to the game'.

In one of the recordings in my collection, Cloughie described scoring goals as the hardest part of the game – and said it always would be, 'That's why you see so many missed every single week. When you go to a football match, you always get half the crowd saying, "How the hell he missed that I'll never know, I could have put that in." But they couldn't have put it in. If they could have put it in, they'd have been in the side instead of being on the terraces.

'In my day, when the centre halves couldn't play, I finished up with 250 goals in 270 games. Now that, by any standards, is a lot of goals. But the game was a lot slower then and it's changed. Now I think I'd get 249.'

Brilliant.

17

A Shovel of Manure

Chatting to John Robertson in March 2023, it still felt surreal that I was talking to a man who'd been instrumental in winning the European Cup, not just once but twice. He was humble, kind and relaxed. Certainly no sign of any ego that needed massaging. No suggestion of any kind of self-importance that can sometimes come with footballing success. I'd arranged to see him before he attended a private event in which a small group of fans joined him for a meal at a Nottingham restaurant.

We spent 20 minutes together in a corner of the restaurant, talking about old times and of course those wonderful days of playing for Brian Clough. I reminded him of how Cloughie used to tell jokes at Robertson's expense (usually about his dishevelled appearance) before going on to praise him as a football genius. 'I really didn't mind that,' Robertson told me, 'because I knew it was all just a bit of fun. I knew that he liked what I did on the pitch and I just wanted to please him.'

Clough had said, 'I called Robbo "the fat man" and all sorts of other names. But put a ball at his feet and he became an artist … the Picasso of our game.'

Robertson described how he craved Clough's approval and felt on top of the world when he received a special signal from the dugout. Clough would put his thumb and forefinger together to form a circle, in a gesture which said, 'That's just perfection, young man.'

But Clough was never impressed with Robertson's time-keeping and would fine him for being late for training. He would suggest that the left-winger would find it cheaper to invest in an alarm clock than to keep paying fines for his tardiness.

'He was always fining me for something,' Robertson told me with a twinkle in his eye. 'He once fined me for not getting off the team bus because I was still reading a book and hadn't heard the instruction. But he was right. It was idiotic of me.'

It wasn't the first time that reading a book had got Robbo into trouble. Determined to get a tan on a sunshine holiday in 1978, he spent too long reading while lying on the beach and suffered with horrendous sunstroke for the remainder of the break.

Throughout our conversation, I was struck by the complete modesty of a man who, in his heyday, should have been hailed as the best player in Europe. He was the Messi, Ronaldo and Mbappé of his time. He still feels the all-conquering Clough teams of 1979 and 1980 never really got the credit they deserved. And he's right of course. Cloughie himself once said, 'They all said it was a flash in the pan. Some flash.'

In some ways, Clough was fortunate that Robertson was on Forest's books when he arrived in 1975. The previous manager, Allan Brown, had offered the Scot to Partick Thistle in a swap deal which eventually fell through. In one of the interviews I found on cassette, Brian actually admitted he was 'lucky' there were already several players in the Forest side who had great potential but hadn't secured a regular starting place under Brown.

Clough later reflected, 'There were five or six players here who people didn't think could play. But once they got with players who *could* play, *they* blossomed. It was like giving John Robertson a shovel of manure. Nobody knew it, but suddenly you give him a shovel of manure and a beautiful flower came up.'

The former *Nottingham Evening Post* journalist John Lawson told me how, soon after Clough's arrival at Forest, Brian had asked him whether there were any potentially talented players he should look out for. The answer: John Robertson.

At the launch of his autobiography, Robertson told me about that valuable recommendation from the other John, who wrote the book with him, 'I wasn't getting a game and Brian didn't know me. But John Lawson was in my corner. When Clough asked if he knew anyone who could play, he suggested me, which brought me to his attention. I then played at Fulham and from then on he knew who I was and I was playing.'

In the run-up to that Fulham match, a newspaper report by Lawson said that Robertson could fill the spot left by the suspended Paul Richardson. The article quoted Clough himself, 'I have seen Robertson in the past and always regarded him as a skilful player. I don't know why but his career seems to have gone flat over the last couple of years.' Lawson wrote that Robertson's 'natural flair would seem to be criminally wasted in the Central League'.

Switched from central midfield to the left wing, Robertson became what team-mate Martin O'Neill described to me as 'the fulcrum' of the side. He was the star of Forest's two European Cup Final victories, setting up the winning goal for Trevor Francis in the first before scoring himself in the second.

Yet Clough admitted that, initially, he had to discourage the Forest supporters from shouting abuse at Robertson, 'He came to see me one Saturday and said, "You've got to get these spectators off my back." There was a certain section of spectators who were giving him some stick before he'd actually touched the ball.'

Brian explained that he walked along the touchline and had what he described as 'a quiet word' with these fans. Now, it's hard to imagine Brian having 'a quiet word' in those circumstances – you'd probably have expected him to use simple but stark terms. 'There was no Anglo-Saxon language,' Clough added. You can then sense the smile on his face as he continued, 'I never used to delve into that [type of language] at that time – not much I didn't!'

The fans needed to be taught about Robertson's real talent, said Clough, 'Once we'd settled the so-called discussion or argument, then he settled down completely.' Repeating one of his favourite theories, he said it was important to focus on a player's strengths rather than his weaknesses, 'We educated them, the fans, to John Robertson because he wanted people to realise what he'd got. All they saw was a little fat lad who couldn't run and they weren't looking at what he *had* got. It's the same with coaches when you're coaching footballers. Bad coaches concentrate on what you haven't got in preference to what you *have* got.' Then, in the style of a lecturer imparting his wisdom to eager students, Clough concluded with this advice, 'You concentrate on what you have got and just niggle away at what you haven't got, and you've got yourself a player.'

Turning the cassette over, I listened as Brian went on to describe how Robertson had developed as a player by performing alongside team-mates who could help him blossom. 'We surrounded him with players who required his skills – he couldn't run for a start and he was about three stone overweight. So we had to get somebody who could run alongside him and who was three stone lighter. We stuck Archie Gemmill alongside him and we had Tony Woodcock, Garry Birtles and Martin O'Neill. John had a special talent so he fitted well into the side.'

Although Clough liked to have a gentle jibe at Robertson's appearance (he once said that Robbo's pair of dirty and well-worn desert boots were in such a state that even the dustbin men refused to take them), the man on the receiving end told me he knew it was only said 'in fun' and that he knew Brian admired his role on the pitch. 'For a man of his stature and reputation in the game to think I was a good player was really, really great,' he said. 'I'm proud to have played for him.'

Defender Colin Barrett remembers playing alongside Robertson on the left, including in the 2-0 victory over Liverpool in the European Cup, in which Barrett scored a wonder goal. He told me, 'Cloughie used to say, "Get the ball and give it to the little so-and-so on the line and we'll go from there." Robbo was one of those players who, no matter what – however tight he was being marked – always made himself available for the ball. He was a talented, talented boy who didn't know his own ability.'

In the Liverpool match, Barrett blocked the ball and decided to continue running forward. A pass to Robertson wasn't an option and when the ball eventually reached the penalty area and came to Barrett from a cushioned header by Tony Woodcock, the left-back fired home a beautiful volley past Ray Clemence. 'I knew I had to score,' Colin told me. 'I was out of position and I knew I'd have been fined for not staying back if the ball hadn't hit the back of the net!'

Forest's first European Cup match on foreign soil was against AEK Athens, who were managed by the Real Madrid and Hungarian legend Ferenc Puskás – a man Robertson had tried to imitate as a youngster, improving his left foot by hitting a ball against a wall. John recalled a hostile atmosphere in Athens, with the home fans setting off flares and creating a cauldron of noise. Cloughie's sister-in-law June had told me for the tribute website how a piece of managerial magic by Brian helped the team cope with the intimidating atmosphere that night. June was in the crowd and remembered how Brian delayed Forest's entrance on to the pitch so the noise had died down a little by the time the players appeared. A 1-1 draw in the first leg was followed by a 5-1 win at home.

Understandably, Robertson said it still annoyed him when some people claimed the modern-day Champions League was harder to win than the European Cup was. In those days, teams didn't get into the competition unless they really were champions of their respective leagues. In the big-money game (or business) of today, sides can finish way behind the domestic champions and still have a chance of lifting the European prize.

It's incredible to think about it now, but Robertson earned £125 a week during the season that Forest won the First Division. That was increased to £225 a week in the year they won the European Cup for the first time. Although the financial rewards were never as large then as they are now for the megastars of today, Robertson is more than content with the adventure he enjoyed alongside Brian Clough at Forest. 'I wouldn't swap what happened in my day for what happens now,' he told me. 'I'm glad I made a career. I wouldn't swap my European Cup medals for a hundred grand a week.'

18

Brian and the Iron Man

Sitting next to each other in front of an expectant audience of football fans, the two men were as formidable together as they were in their professional pomp.

Both neatly dressed, each wearing a smart shirt and tie, it seemed a million years from the days when they worked together and took English football by storm. But as they recalled those golden days, it didn't seem that long ago after all. The memories came flooding back – as did the mutual admiration, which was fascinating to listen to. Especially when Cloughie, well known for calling the shots throughout his management career, pointed to the man sitting on his left and said, 'He used to run the show.'

He was referring to Dave Mackay, also known as the 'Iron Man', who he signed for Derby – against the odds – from Tottenham and re-ignited a playing career which finished with style and further success. It was an inspired signing and one which Clough always said was the best of his entire managerial career.

Clough told the audience at the forum, 'When he was working with me, he ran the place – lock, stock and barrel. The biggest influence he used to have was deciding which day we should come in for training!'

In reality, Mackay's influence went far wider than that of course. The author Norman Giller, who has written many books about his beloved Spurs, told me Clough's signing of Mackay was nothing short of momentous. Giller shed more light on the circumstances surrounding Clough's trip to White Hart Lane to secure Mackay's signature – for which he borrowed Derby chairman Sam Longson's Rolls-Royce.

'Clough was very clever in the way he signed Dave,' said Norman. When the Spurs boss Bill Nicholson agreed that Brian could talk to Dave, the first thing Bill asked was, 'What's the position regarding John O'Hare?' John had signed for Derby from Sunderland, where Cloughie knew him from his work coaching the youth side. But Clough was adamant O'Hare was going nowhere – unlike Mackay, who he was there to see.

'When Cloughie arrived [at White Hart Lane] and was given permission to talk to Dave, he took over Bill Nicholson's office,' said Norman. 'As Dave came into the office, Cloughie stood up and locked the door. He told Dave, "You're not leaving here until you sign that piece of paper which says you're my player." Sure enough, after about an hour – and some very clever negotiating – it was all agreed.'

Mackay had been set to leave Spurs to become assistant manager at Heart of Midlothian, his boyhood club. Clough persuaded him that he could still play an influential role on the pitch at Derby – although perhaps not as active as his fearless and forceful style which had helped Tottenham win the double in 1961, as well as a host of other trophies.

'Dave couldn't believe it,' added Norman. 'He was being told he wouldn't be playing the buccaneering role that he'd played for ten great years at Spurs. Cloughie told him, "You're going to play in defence and I've got a young man called Roy McFarland who you're going to teach how to play the game."' By playing alongside McFarland, Mackay could avoid any stresses on his legs, which were struggling by this time. 'Dave spent a season and a half showing Roy the art of positional play and Roy became one of Europe's great centre-halves,' said Giller, who added that Mackay had also been very shrewd during the transfer talks. 'He squeezed every penny out of them that he could. Cloughie gave him his own column in the match programmes, for which he paid him more money than he was paying any other first-team player – that was even before his wages.'

The addition of Mackay was a vital piece of Clough's Derby jigsaw. 'Dave saw out his career by winning promotion to the First Division and Cloughie was the mastermind of it all,' reflected Giller. 'He knew Dave's legs had gone but that his brain was intact. He used that brainpower to get Derby into the First Division.'

Reflecting on his arrival at the Baseball Ground, Mackay told the football forum, 'When I went to Derby, I was an old guy coming up against young kids. I was 33 years old – [his career was] coming to an end, but I could still do a job. The youngsters who were there helped me, and I helped them.'

In the column for the First Division game against Stoke City in August 1969, Mackay expressed his joy at playing in the top flight again. Derby had enjoyed an unbeaten start to the season, with victory over Ipswich at home and away and draws against Burnley and Coventry.

'How thrilling it is to be playing in front of really big crowds again,' he said. 'I must say that it hardly seems to me that I have ever been out of the First Division, because we also played so many big matches in front of large crowds last season.' The following month, Mackay's recognition of the scale of the support was rewarded when the Baseball Ground attendance reached a record 41,826 for the Rams' 5-0 demolition of Spurs. Nevertheless, he wouldn't be drawn on the idea of it being a successful return to the top flight, neither for himself nor Derby as a club.

'It is amazing how many critics start marking teams down for promotion struggles or honours almost before the players have taken their first breath,' he continued. 'There is a long, long way to go. The "sprinters" often fall by the wayside and the teams with greater strength of character forge through.' Derby finished the season in fourth position. That would have qualified them for the UEFA Cup, but they were denied their first appearance in European football when a joint FA and Football League disciplinary commission found the club guilty of administrative irregularities.

When Clough referred in the forum to Mackay choosing which day the team would train, it was a further sign of his total admiration for the Scotsman. 'After a match, I'd say, "Right, David, what day do you think we should come in training next week?"' At that point there was a huge burst of laughter in the audience, at the thought that Mackay, not Clough, was really in charge.

'It's a true story, because you can ask him,' Clough added, trying to justify the fact he wasn't telling a joke this time.

'Then silence would go round the dressing room and there'd be 12 pairs of eyes all looking at him [Mackay]. He'd got it all worked out. Monday suited him one week, then Tuesday. Then on one occasion I heard Alan Durban say to David, "Tell him Wednesday this week, Dave."' There was more uncontrollable laughter from the audience.

'They're true stories,' Clough insisted, playing to the crowd. 'After the match, I said, "Right, David, what day will suit you then, this week?" He said, "Well, I've got a heavy week, Gaffer." I thought aye-up there's a rabbit up here. He said, "Is there any chance of Wednesday?" And Durban was in the process of getting his head in his boots! I said, "Wednesday will do fine." And we turned-up for training on Wednesday morning and had Sunday, Monday and Tuesday off.

'That was our coaching session. When people asked me when we did our coaching, I said we did it on Monday, Tuesday and Wednesday. Everybody came back much better for it. Come Saturday, we'd have taken *anybody* on.'

But the favours for Mackay didn't stop there. Brian continued, 'He was living in London and I had this daft rule where if you work for someone then you live in the same area. I didn't like people living outside Derby. But David had got his business interests in London and he asked if he could stay in London for a period of time and sort his business out. And I said, "Of course, you can do anything." And I'm standing to attention in his presence! And then I got in the car and I said to myself, "He's a right clever bu**er."'

As well as success on the pitch, Cloughie was grateful to Mackay for something else. Something that money could never buy. He spent hours and hours with young Nigel teaching him how to control and strike a football perfectly. It was like listening to a little bit of footballing history being explained as I played the recording of Brian recalling those special times.

Referring to Nigel, Brian said, 'David Mackay taught him how to play football. That's how much I owe this gentleman.' It was a fantastic moment, as the strong bond between the two men was demonstrated in just a few words.

Cloughie explained that Dave would stay in the Midland Hotel when he was in Derby and – keen to leave his hotel room as soon as possible – he would arrive at the Baseball Ground long before many of his team-mates. Sometimes he got there before Clough himself. During the school holidays Brian would take Nigel with him to the Baseball Ground.

'My bairn used to say, "Is Mr Mackay coming in this morning?" And I'd say, "Yes, he'll be in."'

Nigel would spend hours practising in the wooden shooting box underneath one of the stands, with Mackay giving instructions as they both kicked the ball at a target, which was circular, like the targets used for archery.

'David used to say, "We'll go for the red today or we'll go for the bull." And for hour after hour David used to look after him,' recalled Brian. 'And then of course when David had gone home, he'd be there all day, kicking the ball on his own.'

* * *

If you listen back carefully to the recording of the forum, you can hear Cloughie chuckling to himself when Mackay answers a question about a well-known photograph. It's the one in which Dave is confronting Leeds United's Billy Bremner. Mackay's face is contorted with anger as he grabs Bremner by the scruff of the neck, as if he's about to lift him in the air using just one arm.

The *Daily Mirror* image was taken on the first day of the 1966/67 season during a league match at White Hart Lane. Although it's widely regarded as iconic, Mackay, playing for Spurs at the time, disliked it because he said it made him look like a bully. A member of the audience referred to having a copy of this 'glorious photo' at home and asked Mackay if he was able to repeat what he had said to Bremner at the time.

Guess who responded to the question before Mackay had a chance to speak? Yes, Cloughie. Never a great fan of the way Leeds behaved under Don Revie, Brian was keen to comment on this particular subject, 'Before Dave answers, I'll tell you how many words got through Billy Bremner's mouth … none!' The audience burst out laughing before calming down to hear what Mackay, himself, had to say about the incident.

'It was a very serious occasion,' said Dave, before explaining that he didn't actually pick Bremner up by his shirt, 'Because he's smaller than me.' What riled Mackay was that he had previously broken his leg, not once but twice ('It wasn't broken, it was smashed,' clarified Mackay) and Bremner deliberately moved around Dave to give the leg a kick. 'At that time I was so angry I could have lifted an elephant, never mind Billy,' Mackay told the audience. 'I was so annoyed, I'd never been so annoyed in my life. [I thought that] if he breaks my leg, and it's broken again … but I played for a reasonable time after that.'

Mackay said the incident had happened within the first few minutes of the match. There was a throw-in and Mackay admitted he had pushed Bremner ('we were always fighting'). Bremner fell over and was on all fours before getting up and kicking Mackay's leg. Mackay said, 'It was the dirty Leeds team that Brian talked about – and I agree with him. They were a very good team and could have won a lot more if they hadn't had those players doing silly little things.'

Despite this famous incident, Mackay said he admired Bremner and had attended the former Leeds midfielder's funeral. 'People have asked me a million times [about the photograph]. I was so angry,' said Mackay. 'I don't remember saying anything to him, I really don't.' Then Clough had a laugh to himself as his former captain added, 'He never said anything back.'

Both players escaped a yellow card after the confrontation, possibly because it was early in the game. Mackay usually conducted himself responsibly on – and off – the pitch. However, I found a newspaper cutting from December 1969 which described how he had received a rare booking in a match against Newcastle United. His offence? Kicking the ball away after two other players had been involved in a foul. Mackay told the media afterwards, 'It will never happen to me again. The last time I was booked was so long ago I can't even remember it and it will be a lot longer before that happens again. Take my word for that.' The headline of the newspaper report was 'Dave vows: No more bookings'. It was a pledge that pleased his manager. 'Dave has assured me that he won't be in trouble again. And I know he won't,' said Brian, before adding, 'I don't like having my players booked.'

The issue of yellow cards being dished out like confetti was debated during the forum and Mackay told the audience that he thought the game had 'gone a little bit soft'. He also reckoned that referees were not strong enough to stand up to abuse from players. 'I see yellow cards given for every little challenge,' said Mackay. 'Referees were a lot stronger in the past.' He then referred to a top-flight player who was often seen swearing at the officials. 'In the old days – or the golden old days – if you swore at a referee you'd get a card. But these guys slag the referees off, they're always moaning and groaning and I don't think the referees of today are strong enough.'

* * *

The bond of respect between Clough and Mackay surfaced again when Brian was asked about leaving Derby in 1973 and whether he had hoped that, in time, there would be the opportunity to return. In answering, Clough referred to Mackay, his successor at the Baseball Ground, in the type of glowing terms that are well worth putting on the record. A member of the audience said that when Clough appeared on the Michael Parkinson chat show after resigning, he appeared sure he would eventually return to the Baseball Ground. Brian was asked, 'How confident were you of a return?'

He replied, 'It hadn't sunk in with me that I was going to leave altogether, because you always hang on to something you like, irrespective of how strongly you feel. It felt like I'd been at Derby for 25 years instead of five years, and I thought, "You never know, I might get back there again." But it didn't work out like that and you got a better manager instead.' You could sense Mackay puffing out his chest with pride on hearing those special words.

At the time of Clough's resignation from Derby, a huge public campaign began to have him reinstated as manager. Colin Shields, who became a close friend of Brian's during his Forest days, joined what was known as the 'Protest Movement'. Colin told me about one particular meeting at which a mysterious visitor decided to attend.

'I went to several meetings of the Protest Movement, including one at the Kings Hall when there was a lot of gossip about a man sitting at the back, in the shadows. There were whispers that it was a spy from the club. But it later emerged that it was actually Brian – and he made a quick exit when he suspected he had been spotted.

'In my desperation to find any way I could to campaign for Brian's reinstatement, I joined what was known as the Executive Club. I hoped I could pull a few strings behind the scenes. For just a few pounds extra, the Executive Club ran special trips to away matches – I would travel first class on the train alongside directors and other executives. I thought that if I could get amongst that group of people, I might be able to influence Brian's return. But it was like trying to fight your way through a brick wall.'

When a protest march was held before a home match against Leicester, Colin was among the crowd. 'There was a fantastic atmosphere during the march, with people carrying placards and banners, but I think there should have been a bigger turn-out,' said Colin. 'If 80 per cent of the fans who turned out for the game that afternoon had taken part in the march beforehand it would have had such a big impact. While we were walking through the streets behind the band, onlookers were shouting at us, "Why don't you grow up?" and, "You're being stupid – it's nothing to do with you!" They seemed steeped in the old attitude that you can't do anything – that you couldn't try to change things.

'There was talk of the players possibly going on strike. They wanted to get involved in the campaign, but they remained very professional and their role as players came first. The minute that Dave Mackay returned to become manager, we knew we were finished.'

When I spoke to Alan Hinton, he told me how strongly the Derby team felt about the situation, 'I wrote a resignation letter on behalf of the players. We planned to go to Majorca and not play against Leicester. But the guy in charge of the Professional Footballers' Association phoned our captain Roy McFarland and said if we didn't play the game there was a chance of getting a lifetime ban. So we played the game.'

It wasn't long before Mackay left his job as Nottingham Forest manager and succeeded Brian at Derby. One of the questions during the forum was focussed on this turn of events, 'How did you turn the players around to be on your side?' Mackay was direct in his reply. He said it had been rubbish (or a similar word) for the press to report that the players had refused to go training when he became Derby boss. The players *had* gone training, he said, although he had faced a difficult situation. The fact that he had been a successful Derby player was an important factor, 'If any other manager had gone in there, they would have failed and Brian would have been back in his job, for sure. I knew the players, I'd been away only two or three years and I slowly turned them around.'

From the players' point of view, Hinton told me they were impressed with Mackay from the moment he addressed them, soon after he arrived. 'We had a meeting on the Monday morning and Dave Mackay made a brilliant speech. He said, "Gentlemen, I know you don't want me as your manager, but I want this job." He said he'd have been sick to the stomach if he'd read in the newspaper that somebody else had got the job when he'd already been offered it. He told us, "I need you to know that I know you all and I enjoyed playing with you – and Brian Clough *did* resign." And in the end, he [Mackay] won the day. Once we started to roll under Dave, we won the division again.'

Mackay told the forum that Brian had been a hard act to follow, and said, 'But I got on with the job.' There was even a Clough-type comment which prompted instant applause from the audience, 'I know I did a very good job there.' He said he didn't worry about criticism and had felt he was well-liked during his second spell at Derby because he had been a successful player. Referring to the man sitting on his right, Mackay added, 'He did resign and if I hadn't taken the job they would have given it to someone else.'

* * *

'We must win for David's sake.' Those were Cloughie's words back in September 1969 as Derby were due to face Spurs. Clough's decision to remind people about the importance of winning the game against Mackay's former club only added to the fans' expectations. A record crowd of nearly 42,000 crammed into the ground to watch a special piece of history, as the man who had enjoyed such an incredible career at the London club – winning First Division and FA Cup medals – was now in a newly promoted side aiming to beat them. 'I had some great times with Spurs, but I play for Derby County now,' said Mackay before the game. 'I shall be the proudest man in England when I lead the lads out.' Clough said the game promised to be a good spectacle, 'And I know our lads will be giving everything for David's sake. He wants to win this match more than anything.'

Not only did Derby win for Dave, they demolished Spurs 5-0. Despite winning their previous four away matches, Tottenham were reduced to 'an inept shambles' according to the *Derby Evening Telegraph*. Sports editor George Edwards summed it up in his report when he wrote, 'It wasn't a match, it was a massacre.' After the game, the Spurs manager Bill Nicholson said Derby had humiliated his team. 'They are very talented and they don't just run, they know when to run and where,' he acknowledged. Nicholson said Mackay was an inspiration and a credit to the game. Mackay himself said he was happy for his team, 'Not because it was Spurs we beat but because you can't be anything but happy when you are in a team which plays like that. It is the best we have played since I came here.'

Not surprisingly, Nicholson admitted he was sorry he had let Mackay leave, 'When I let Dave go, neither he nor I suspected his move would turn out like this. But good luck to him. I wish I had six Dave Mackays in my side, then I wouldn't have any worries.'

Clough had the last word, telling the media, 'All I can say is that we are going to shock a lot more people before the season is through.'

* * *

There was a lovely moment of humour during the football forum when Clough and Mackay talked about how they'd aged over the years. Here's the exchange:

DM, 'We're both the same age.'

BC, 'To be fair, looking at the pair of us, you've worn well.'

DM, 'I remember Brian when he first signed me from Tottenham. I was 33 years old. He was the same age but he only looked about 19. But now he's caught me up.' Cue instant laughter from the audience.

BC, 'I'm actually past you [even more crowd laughter]. One of his children who lives with him said, "I'm sick and tired of seeing the photograph of Cloughie on our piano." David's got a photograph of us both and it's on his piano. His bairn said to him, "Are you lying Dad? Is he definitely younger than you?"'

DM, 'The photo is under one of the [piano] legs now.'

19

It Started With a Kiss

The newspaper headline marked the publication of my first Cloughie book. 'It Started With a Kiss' declared page five of the *Nottingham Evening Post* and the cutting, from 4 December 2008, is still part of my collection. It referred to the moment when Brian gave me a big hug and a kiss on the cheek. Over the years I've loved hearing stories about those moments when he momentarily let his guard down and showed a softer side of his no-nonsense public persona.

Even his former players couldn't escape the classic Cloughie kiss. Although in the case of European Cup winner Viv Anderson, the tables were turned. Anderson was the captain of Sheffield Wednesday when Clough's Forest visited Hillsborough. He told me how the special request to give Brian a smacker on the cheek came about, 'As a tradition, the captain always takes the team out for the warm-up, but I hated warm-ups, so I was out there for only five minutes. I'd take them out, have a run and then get back into the dressing room. As I'm coming off the pitch, Mr Clough is sitting on his own in the dugout, where there are lots of Sheffield Wednesday fans.

'So I said, "Hello, Mr Clough," and he says, "Come here, young man." I said, "I've got to get inside now." He goes, "Come here." So I go over to him and he says, "Give us a kiss." So I had to kiss him on the cheek and then scampered down the tunnel to get to the dressing room as quickly as I could.' Anderson may have been a little embarrassed, but it showed the admiration Cloughie had for many of his former players – plus the fans loved it. Anderson still remembers the cheers from the supporters around the dugout.

* * *

Another of Cloughie's European Cup winners remembers being on the receiving end of a Clough kiss in front of his team-mates, even though he – like Anderson – had left Forest and was playing for the opposition.

Tony Woodcock left the City Ground to join Cologne in Germany and then came back to the UK to play for Terry Neill's Arsenal. For four seasons he was the Gunners' top scorer. After a match which Forest lost, there was a knock on the door of the away dressing room. It was Brian Clough. Woodcock thought to himself that he should get to the door quickly, but Clough had already stepped just inside the dressing room. 'I walk over to him and he puts his arms around me and kisses me,' recalled Woodcock, in an interview clip on the *Local Heroes* DVD (2023). Clough said just four words, 'Well done, young man,' and walked away. The Arsenal players couldn't believe what they had just witnessed and gave Woodcock some friendly banter.

The significance of the gesture has never been lost on the former England international, 'I think it was to show that we'd "got on" over the years. A show of respect. And I was really pleased he took me in his arms and gave me a kiss.'

* * *

In my case, I think the Cloughie kiss was a gesture of pure appreciation, mixed with memories of some magical times. I'd read in a local newspaper that he was going to be the special guest at a fete in Derbyshire, where I was working at the time.

Although he'd retired from football management, he was still keen to help the local community by appearing at a fundraising event. The reason I went along was to ask him to sign a wonderful glossy black and white photo I'd ordered from the *Nottingham Evening Post*. It was a large and unusual picture of Cloughie in the dressing room with his victorious Nottingham Forest team after they had just secured their place in the 1991 FA Cup Final.

The photo was a great memory of a sunny day at Villa Park when I watched Forest beat West Ham in the semi-final. Cloughie didn't often invite the media into his dressing room, but on this occasion he had. The photographer captured a classic scene, with Brian sitting in his dressing gown, legs outstretched and arms folded, alongside his players and backroom staff. My plan was to get everyone on the photo to sign it.

I spent several weeks waiting outside the Forest dressing room after training sessions, in the hope of asking the various players to add their names. And they all did. The likes of Roy Keane, Stuart Pearce, Des Walker, Brian Laws and Nigel

Clough, who is pictured with a towel round his waist. The backroom staff signed it too, but the one signature which remained missing was that of Cloughie himself.

So that morning I headed for the local fete, carrying the photo in a large brown padded envelope. It was a fairly low-key event and there was a small number of people waiting with me for Cloughie's autograph. He was sitting behind a small table, signing everything that was presented to him, from books to scraps of paper. He took time to speak to everyone as we queued. I waited at the back of the queue, watching him interact with each visitor. At one point there was a screaming child accompanying one of the people who was asking for an autograph. The screaming continued. 'Now then, be quiet!' Cloughie barked, pointing to the noisy young culprit. 'Don't worry, I'm only being rude!' he added with a wry smile.

Then it was my turn. I hoped he was in a good mood so he could take time to appreciate the photo I was about to show him. I carefully pulled the image out of the envelope, wondering exactly what his reaction would be when he saw it. His eyes lit up as he gazed across that dressing room scene, as if the memories were flooding back. Looking more closely, he could see all his players had signed it.

'I wondered if you could sign this for me please, Mr Clough. Yours is the only signature I'm missing,' I said, my hands trembling as I handed him the pen. 'My pleasure, young man,' came the reply, as he carefully started to add his signature.

Handing back the pen, he took one more look at the photo. 'Happy days,' he said, nodding. 'Thanks Mr Clough, you've made my day,' I said, even though my mouth was dry with nerves. At that point, he looked up at me and got out of his chair. 'Young man, you've made my day too,' he said and stepped towards me. He opened his arms and gave me a huge bear hug and a kiss on the cheek.

Looking back, I'm glad that photo brought back some good memories for him. For me, it still does. I had the photo framed and I see it every day.

* * *

When the world's media descended on the City Ground in May 1993 for Cloughie's final home league match, one interview stood out from the rest. At the end of an emotional conversation with BBC commentator Barry Davies, Brian looked truly touched by the interviewer's kindness and gave him a big hug. It was another indication of the softer side of Cloughie, often hidden from the cameras.

Reflecting on his encounters with the Miracle Manager, Davies told a BBC documentary in 2010 how much he valued the time he'd spent with Brian, along with the special memories he'd left behind. 'He's the only manager who's kissed me in public,' said Davies. 'I'm not alone though, he'd kissed a few other people.'

Davies continued with a wonderful tribute, 'Time in his company would be provoking, interesting and fun. And I think I'm a better person for having known him – and I think that applies to a lot of other people.'

20

Cloughie and Archie

When I interviewed Archie Gemmill for my *Green Jumper* podcast, I told him how Cloughie had described him as one of his best signings. The reply was superb – and was delivered with a timing of which Clough himself would have been proud.

'He was a good judge,' said Gemmill.

Listening to one of my rare Clough recordings – a conversation from 2002 – Brian spoke about the man who served him so brilliantly as a human dynamo in the midfield at Derby and Forest, and later as a loyal coach at the City Ground. When it comes to classic quotes, this is another belter, 'I put a Nottingham Forest tape on last night and I watched Archie Gemmill. And I didn't know he was THAT good. And I watched this tape of various matches and he kept winning the ball. He kept running 45 yards and he kept scoring the odd goal. I didn't remember him scoring goals. He kept doing everything. I thought, "Blow me, you were worth another five quid a week."'

Personally, I also loved watching Gemmill play. His lung-splitting run against Arsenal – when he gathered the ball in his own half, released it to Peter Withe and burst forward to finish the move with a wonderful goal – will live long in the memory. It was voted *Match of the Day*'s Goal of the Season in 1978.

That goal summed up Gemmill's grit and determination, combined with silky skill, on a football pitch. When he played, he was a winner, pure and simple. He once said, 'There are no prizes for coming second.'

His former Derby County team-mate Alan Hinton told me that Archie played better when he was riled – in other words, he needed to be really fired up when he crossed that white line. Clough and Peter Taylor knew which buttons to press. 'Archie was a tough kid from Scotland and I'm sure Brian enjoyed winding him up,' said Hinton when he spoke to me from his Seattle home in the United States. 'The more he insulted Archie, the better he played. I'm sure Brian and Peter used to sit together and say, "How can we make Archie mad? How can we make Archie really angry?" Archie covered every blade of grass and every mud hole. I remember one time his boot came off in the mud and he just picked it up, put it back on and continued to run.'

Speaking to Gemmill, you can see how Clough's provocation had the desired effect, 'There were times when I was at Derby and I'd get rollicked at half-time. I thought I'd played well, but at half-time I'd get slaughtered. Things like, "You're useless, why did we sign you?" I didn't think it was needed and some of it wasn't very nice.'

I asked him if he felt he could challenge Clough and stand up for himself. 'I had my say,' said Gemmill. 'If you feel you've done well, you might as well stick up for yourself. If they said, "You're obviously useless," I'd say something like, "Well, what game are you watching?" I used to think I was playing well, but he always said that if he didn't stay on top of me, I wouldn't become a better player.'

All these years later, I still got the distinct impression that this amazing player remains tough on himself when he looks back at his career. For example, his wonder goal for Scotland against the Netherlands in the 1978 World Cup is still remembered for its solo brilliance. But when I asked him whether he had a favourite goal (was the one against Arsenal just as good?) his reply focussed on what he regarded as a lack of goals overall.

'To be fair, I never scored a lot of goals in my career. If I look back, that would be the one thing that stands out. Per game, my goal ratio was pretty poor. In fact it was c**p. It would have been nice if I'd have scored 130 or 140 goals or something like that in my career. I got about 50.'

Putting the goal count aside, the one thing you couldn't criticise Gemmill for was any lack of desire or effort. In another interview he summed up a philosophy which would apply to the man himself, 'In general, the people who give 100 per cent the whole of the time will eventually be a success.' And it was that steely determination which must have attracted Clough and Taylor to sign him from Preston – snatching him from under the nose of Everton.

The young Scot wanted to talk to the Goodison club and he tried to put the pair off. But they were determined to get his signature. Clough wouldn't leave until the deal was done.

'He [Clough] decided he was going to sleep outside in the car,' said Gemmill. 'But my wife invited him in and he stayed the night. She cooked him breakfast in the morning ... and I ended up signing in the morning.'

In an interview for RamsTV in 2020, Gemmill explained more about the background to the transfer, 'Alan Ball (senior), who was manager at Preston at the time, called me in and said there had been a bid in from Derby County and that we should have a listen to what they had to say.

'I said I wasn't interested at all because all I have to do is sign at Everton. He said to just go and meet him to see if he is like what he is on television. So, I went and had the meeting and the following day I was signed for Derby.

'The thing that eventually got me to sign for Derby was when he [Clough] was sitting at the kitchen table having breakfast, because he stayed at the house that night. He said to me, "Let's get down to facts. What is the midfield at Everton?"

'I said, "Ball, Harvey and Kendall." He said, "What chance have you got playing for them? If you sign here, you play for Derby on Saturday." That was it, I didn't even know what I was getting.'

Gemmill said Clough and Taylor were highly persuasive. 'If they got something between their teeth, they wouldn't let it go. They said it was the final piece in the jigsaw to win the championship. And that's what happened. We won the championship that year.'

An archive newspaper cutting from the *Liverpool Echo* indicated just how close Gemmill had been to joining Everton – and how crucial Clough's personal intervention had been. The Everton manager at the time was Harry Catterick, who the *Echo* described as 'one of football's classic cloak-and-dagger merchants in the transfer market'. Looking back at his career, Catterick revealed how a fee had been agreed with Preston. Catterick lived at Southport at the time and was a frequent spectator at Preston matches. He spotted Gemmill's energetic displays and became determined to get his man.

According to Catterick, the agreement that Preston would sell Gemmill to Everton was even put in writing. He told the *Echo*, 'It would never have stood up in a court of law, but it was an agreement between two clubs.' However, the phone rang in the early hours of the morning and Ball told Catterick that Derby were also interested in the young midfielder. When the Everton boss pointed out that an agreement had been signed, Ball replied that Clough was with him at that moment and wouldn't leave until he had Gemmill's signature. Catterick continued, 'I told him that as far as I was concerned Gemmill was coming to Everton, but it was his decision. And in the end Preston accepted Derby's offer for him.'

Gemmill later followed Clough to the City Ground. But their relationship soured for a while after the Scot was left out of the line-up for the European Cup Final in 1979. The decision led to his departure from Forest the following season.

Speaking on Brian Tansley's *Matchday Programme* on BBC Radio Nottingham, before Clough passed away, Gemmill said he often visited his old gaffer because he lived nearby, 'We reminisce about the old times and the subject always comes up – about leaving me out of the European Cup Final.'

Gemmill said he had been 'more than upset' by the decision to leave him out of the match against Malmö. And he still had strong feelings about it.

'I still think he was most certainly in the wrong. But he keeps saying to me, "What was the score?" He always has the last word,' Gemmill added with a laugh.

He said he had been injured in the semi-final but had been promised by Clough and Taylor that he would be in the final if he proved his fitness.

'As far as I was concerned, I had proved my fitness, but I was left out. I made my feelings known to both of them,' Gemmill said.

In my interview with Gemmill for *Green Jumper*, he said that not only did he have to deal with the bitter disappointment of not playing in the European Cup Final, but afterwards he was told to clean Clough's hotel room. Listening to him recount what happened, I shook my head in sympathy for how he must have felt at the time. 'You've just got to bite the bullet,' he added.

On the other side of the story, an interview that Cloughie gave to journalist Keith Daniell in his retirement showed how difficult the decision had been to leave out Gemmill and Martin O'Neill from that 1979 final. 'They both genuinely thought, momentarily, that I was kidding,' said Clough, when he recalled the moment he told the pair that they weren't playing against Malmö. 'It's not easy to tell a guy who you're very close to for nine months of the year, and you look on them as sons, that they're not playing in the pinnacle of their football career, the European Cup. Archie just got up and walked away. It took him about a month to talk to me – or even acknowledge me – never mind talk to me. Martin came round a bit quicker ... but they were hard things [to do] in the European Cup.'

Gemmill was transferred to Birmingham City the following season. When I showed him my letter in *Shoot!* magazine from February 1981, saying that his experience and skill – like that of Ian Bowyer – would be missed from the Forest side, and that Clough and Taylor had made an error in selling him, a smile flashed across his face. 'That's a long time ago,' he said.

'But you *were* missed, make no mistake about it,' I said. Gemmill admitted he didn't enjoy his time at Birmingham and our conversation switched to his return to the City Ground in 1984 as part of Cloughie's coaching staff. It was a highly successful spell for him, as he helped to bring through many great young players. He reflected on some 'wonderful times' working for Brian again.

'I'll remember him as a terrific person first and foremost,' he told me. 'People see him as a bighead or a loudmouth, but he had a great belief in his own ability and he proved it to everybody. He could turn a very average player into a special player. He had a fantastic way of making people become better.' And Gemmill stressed that Brian helped many people away from football too. He would visit frail pensioners and help others, away from the spotlight. 'If you ask many people about him, they'll say, "He was a great manager," but they don't talk about the other half of him – because he did an awful lot for charity.'

Having worked so closely with Brian, and becoming a valued confidante, I wondered whether Gemmill considered himself to have been a friend of Cloughie. In Keith Daniell's interview, Clough refers to Gemmill as 'a dear friend'. I also remember Martin O'Neill saying that Brian 'loved Archie dearly' as a friend.

'You saw the softer side of him [Brian], do you think you became a friend?' I asked Gemmill at the end of our chat.

'Ooh, I don't think anybody was ever a friend,' he replied, with a little laugh in his voice.

'Well, he liked your company,' I added, to which Gemmill agreed. Again, the incredibly talented Scot was being tough on himself. But perhaps that's what made him such an amazing player.

21

Fantasy Football

Despite Archie Gemmill being left out of the 1979 European Cup Final line-up, he *was* included in Cloughie's Nottingham Forest 'Dream Team'.

Long before Fantasy Football became so popular, back in 2001 Brian was asked to pick his ultimate Reds first XI, from all the players he worked with at the City Ground.

'Picking my best team used to come easy to me, but this was different,' he said. 'When you think of all the names who have played for Old Big 'Ead down the years, the list is almost endless.'

Clough said it was fascinating to reflect on his years at the City Ground and the players he worked with. As he looked through the names and old photographs, he admitted, 'The memories came flooding back and left the odd lump in the throat.'

THE DREAM TEAM:

Peter Shilton: 'He was as important to the side as anyone who scored a brilliant goal.'

Viv Anderson: 'There were not many better sights in the game than seeing Viv gliding forward from his right-back position.'

Stuart Pearce: 'At his peak he was awesome – there is no other word for it.'

Des Walker: 'He was a dream for a manager to work with because he hardly ever had a bad game.'

Kenny Burns: 'He could create and score goals as well as defend like a colossus.'

Roy Keane: 'He is a fantastic competitor, heads the ball better than most centre-halves, certainly tackles better and scores goals like strikers.'

John McGovern: 'He had tremendous stamina and a temperament that could survive anything anyone could do to him on a football field.'

Archie Gemmill: 'He never gave less than his maximum and his pace, movement and tackling ability were astonishing.'

John Robertson: 'If you gave him a square yard of grass to work in he was dynamite and for years he was our genius.'

Trevor Francis: 'He added a sparkle to any team that he played for and that goal in Munich will put his name up in Forest lights forever.'

Garry Birtles: 'He never gave up even when the ball was a yard out of play – and his ability with his head, and particularly his left foot, turned him into one of the best strikers of his era.'

Summing up his Forest Fantasy Football selection, Cloughie concluded, 'If you had the team I picked together now at the peak of their game, it might be worth a bob or two. I'd certainly have a flutter on them winning the league.'

But what about some of the brilliant players he didn't include? It reminded me of his admission during Keith Daniell's trophy room interview that it was difficult telling a loyal player that they wouldn't appear in one of the most important matches of their lives, the European Cup Final. Omitting Martin O'Neill and Archie Gemmill from that first XI in Munich was harder than he expected.

Nevertheless, when talking about his Dream Team selection, Clough said, 'It never bothered me upsetting players by leaving them out. Bill Shankly always used to say "pick your best team" and if you do that with total honesty then nobody can have any gripes.

'But I must admit to feeling a little bit uneasy – I must be going soft in my old age – at leaving out some players whose contribution to Nottingham Forest's success over the years was nothing short of fantastic.'

Looking through the names he'd chosen, Clough added, 'It's that good a team my son can't get in it – and he's the second-highest scorer in the history of the club. I think he's entitled to ask if there is a place for him on the bench!'

So, who were his substitutes? These were the five players he selected: Hans van Breukelen, Larry Lloyd, Ian Bowyer, Martin O'Neill and Nigel. 'I couldn't overlook my son for a place on the bench, even if the competition included the likes of Tony Woodcock,' said Brian. 'He got more stick from me than any other player but came bouncing back and always did his job to the best of his ability.'

Talking of substitutes, Clough told a radio programme in 2004 that he was always reluctant to bring on a substitute. 'I hated using subs for various reasons,' he said. 'If I was set on a formation, I had great faith in the fact that I'd picked the right team in the first place. So I was never keen on subs.' But was that still the case if a player was injured and needed to be replaced? 'I used to throw people back on if they were injured as well,' he admitted, recalling how Frank Clark suffered a nasty gash on his shin at Wembley. 'He showed me at half-time and he said, "What am I going to do?" I said you're going back on, simple as that. At Wembley? You don't come off injured.' Unless, of course, you're Paul Gascoigne and are stretchered off, despite launching yourself into some of the most reckless challenges you'll ever see in an FA Cup Final and avoid a red card.

Cloughie also talked about the tactic of making substitutions late in a match to effectively 'kill the game'. It's something he was strongly against. 'We'd have to change the rules because they are using them to waste time, there's no doubt about that,' he said. 'They're bringing them on in the last five minutes to kill the game.' He said it was all very well putting additional time into the match to make up for the minutes lost during the substitutions, but the real problem was about stifling the momentum of the game.

'The game goes dead for a full minute,' he argued. 'People relax and reorganise, depending on the state of the game.' Perhaps substitutes should be banned during the last 15 minutes of a match, he wondered, but what would happen if a player was genuinely injured? A radio listener suggested that, in those cases, most teams that go down to ten players are tougher to break down than those with the full quota of 11. 'Yes, that is a theory,' responded Cloughie, 'but don't lay too much store on that. A good 11 always beats a good ten.'

And that reminds me of a match in which Clough's Forest were playing Crystal Palace. During the second half, Brian took off Steve Hodge without replacing him with a substitute. Garry Thompson, who was playing for Palace, told me how their manager Steve Coppell was left fuming by the decision. Garry, speaking on *Green Jumper*, was more philosophical about it. 'Well, it's Brian Clough, isn't it?' he said. 'Sometimes you've just got to take it.'

22

Churchill, Thatcher and ... Clough

Deep in the BBC TV archives, the legendary chat show host Michael Parkinson made an incredibly insightful comment during an interview with Brian Clough.

Cloughie had been deftly avoiding a tricky question, in the same way that he would sidestep an opposing defender when he was playing as a centre-forward.

'Brian, you're throwing a red herring,' Parkinson told him. 'You're always very clever. You'd make a marvellous politician because you don't answer the question.'

If you look back at some of the answers given during the Cloughie phone-ins I've already documented in this book, you'd have to agree. At other times, he was spot-on when answering a question – and sometimes too honest for his own good.

But the suggestion of Clough having the potential to be a great politician is one that still intrigues me. His plain speaking and championing of social justice for working people would certainly have made him a popular candidate and an uncompromising opponent.

In a 1972 interview, he was asked about his earliest ambitions away from the world of football. 'I'd got visions of putting the world right early doors,' he said, referring to when he was in his early 20s and 'wasting my time' doing national service. It was at that point in his life that he realised that entering politics was the way to do it. 'That was very evident in my early thoughts,' he added.

Clough also revealed that he had been offered a chance at standing for a parliamentary seat when he was still playing football. This is long before speculation gathered pace in the 1970s and 1980s about him possibly standing to become a member of parliament. I'm still amazed to think that if those initial political approaches had been successful, while he was still scoring goals on a regular basis, the world would have been deprived of the most incredible and charismatic football manager ever known. But we could have seen a powerful and passionate politician.

Brian was approached about becoming a Labour candidate in Richmond, Yorkshire, in 1964. Although a Conservative stronghold, it was an area close to his hometown of Middlesbrough. He was still at Sunderland at the time, where he was coaching the youth players following his own injury. Apparently, manager Alan Brown persuaded him to stick to football.

'I didn't think it was right to take it at that particular time,' he told the interviewer. However, he was willing to reconsider the prospect of fighting an election to become an MP many years later. It was August 1972 and Clough had won the First Division championship with Derby County just a few months before. The European Cup beckoned, but he later admitted that if the political calendar had been different, he would have been tempted to enter the fray of a general election. He explained that if a national poll had been three months away, instead of 18 months to two years, it would have been a serious consideration. He said, 'If an election came up and if I was asked to stand for parliament and the situation was different to what it is now, then I could quite easily say, "OK, let's have a go."'

Clough was then asked what aspects of life he would want to put right, if he had become an MP at that time. 'I am not Left, I am extreme Left in certain things – and that is where the whole story would begin,' he said. Was he a Communist, asked the interviewer. Clough said he'd been to Russia and definitely wouldn't want to live there, adding, 'My own type of Communism is fine.'

Many years later, in an interview with Brian Moore, Clough was asked about his socialist beliefs. 'I think socialism comes from the heart and I think I've been lucky and I've got what I've got,' he said. 'I've made a few bob, I've got a car, I've got a nice house and [wagging his finger] I don't see any reason why everybody shouldn't have that.

'People who I've met sometimes with a few bob and have "got on" don't think everybody else should have a few bob and "get on" – and I think the opposite. I think everybody can have it. That's where socialism comes from. I think everybody should have a book, I think everybody should have a nice classroom to go to. Everybody should have the same opportunities.'

Clough once told a reporter from the French magazine *ONZE*, 'I'm a socialist and I have been since I was 20. Possibly I'm more socialist now than ever. You think it's a paradox to be a socialist and drive a Mercedes 280 SE and earn big money? Everyone's entitled to his opinion. But you've only got to open your eyes to find reinforcement for your beliefs.'

Indeed, it was his belief in helping what he considered to be good causes that led him to take part in demonstrations outside an MP's office. The former Rushcliffe MP and Conservative chancellor Ken Clarke, now Lord Clarke, told me how Cloughie would take an enthusiastic part in protests outside his constituency office in West Bridgford. It's a building which is just a short walk from Nottingham Forest's City Ground. The demonstrations would be held on Saturday mornings, when the MP was holding his regular surgery for constituents. Clough's Forest would be playing at home in the afternoon. Perhaps he considered it a good 'warm-up' for the passion of a football match.

'Each week he'd turn up with a different Labour group, different banners and a different cause,' said Lord Clarke. 'They would shout and march and then go away again.' Knowing Brian well, Ken decided to meet him at the ground and express his concern about what was happening. 'It was intimidating my constituents who were trying to explain their problems to me. Some of the old ladies got quite frightened by it.' The experienced MP had no hesitation in confronting the larger-than-life Clough. He told me, 'I spoke to him at the ground and asked him to stop it. I said, "Pack it in, Brian. If you don't, the team's not doing that well at the moment and I'll try to get some fans together and we'll hold a demo outside the ground before matches."' The two men joked about the situation and it seems that a friendly truce was agreed.

While Clough and Clarke were certainly on the opposite ends of the political spectrum, they were on the same side when it came to football. The politician, also the former home secretary, described Brian as the best postwar football manager in the country. He said Clough's record in club management put him head and shoulders above the rest. And that includes the likes of Sir Alex Ferguson. 'If you or I had a go at managing Manchester United we might get the odd trophy with all that money,' Ken told me.

I was also surprised when he said that Brian had been offered the opportunity of a parliamentary seat in the East Midlands. When the Labour Party was looking for a candidate to stand in the Leicestershire seat of Loughborough, apparently Clough was sounded out for it. 'He could have become a Labour MP if he'd won Loughborough, which was quite winnable for the Labour Party,' said Lord Clarke, who reckoned that the Master Manager was 'very wise' to turn down the opportunity of sitting in the House of Commons. 'He wouldn't have enjoyed being an MP. It would have been quite entertaining having Brian there, but I think he would have found the whole place utterly bewildering and it wasn't him.'

An interview with the BBC's David Coleman in 1973 helps to shed some light on the reason why Clough didn't take the plunge into the world of Westminster.

Brian said he felt strongly about politics, but was hugely disillusioned about politicians, 'I look at the government, whether it's the government we've got at the moment or the last government, and we seem to be faced with the same politicians year after year. So it's a safe assumption they've made a mess of it.' He said it was difficult to find any solution to the problem of securing a competent government, 'The only satisfaction I get from the situation is the fact it was arrived at through a democracy.' He said he was still committed to the principles of the Labour Party – although not as a member of the party – and the principles of socialism.

'I'm a little bit disillusioned about politics,' said Clough. 'Actually, not a little bit, I'm a lot disillusioned.' He went on to talk about how politicians in general were viewed suspiciously for not really telling the truth, when compared to people in other walks of life.

I found another archive interview in which Clough was equally scathing about politicians who sought re-election, having failed to put things right in the first place.

'They come back to us, having made such a mess of it, and say "put us back there again" and I find this incredible. They have the gall to knock on your door and tell us that we're in trouble, there are problems and we're all going to have to pull our belts in – and I've paid them, or contributed to them, to put it right.

'We pay their wages and they make such a mess of it and then they come back and ask us to do it all again. You've either got to be as thick as hell to do that – or a very talented man.'

Those comments, which are still relevant today, came in another BBC TV interview, this time with Sir David Frost in November 1974.

Nevertheless, Cloughie had no hesitation in asking for a favour from a politician if he thought it would help his football club. Lord Clarke told me how Brian would occasionally approach him when he needed assistance in securing a work permit or visa for an overseas player.

'For a time in the late 1980s I was a minister at the Department of Employment with some overall responsibility for work permits, when Brian complained to me about the refusal of a permit for a Swedish player he had signed,' he said.

It turned out that the application had been dealt with by a member of staff who was new to the role. In fact it was her first day in the job in that particular division.

'She had sent him a standard letter refusing a work permit in the absence of evidence that no suitable unemployed British citizen was available to fill the post,' explained Lord Clarke. 'The letter told Brian Clough that the best evidence would be produced if he advertised the vacant midfield position in the local newspaper at least three times and could prove that no suitable applicant was available.'

You can imagine what Cloughie said when he telephoned Ken Clarke to express his annoyance. 'He was being told that he'd have to offer this key role to someone from the local dole queue. I will leave his views to your imagination!'

The intended signing of an established international player did eventually go ahead, because it complied with the rules for professional footballers. It followed the failure of Clough's attempt to secure the signature of England's Glenn Hoddle, who had chosen to go to France instead.

'The work permit was granted,' said Lord Clarke, 'and some unfortunate unemployed lad in Nottingham was deprived of the opportunity of having a go at a midfield role in one of the best football clubs in England at that time!'

* * *

Whatever your own personal politics, when it comes to naming historic figures from the world of Westminster, Churchill and Thatcher will be among them. And who'd have thought that the name Clough could have given them a run for their money, even if the Churchill I'm referring to is Sir Winston's grandson?

After giving Clough the chance to contest a massive Conservative majority in Richmond, Surrey, the Labour Party offered him the opportunity to fight the seat of Stretford in Manchester, where Sir Winston's grandson held a much smaller 4,000 majority for the Tories. It made Brian think seriously about becoming an MP. The idea of taking on young Winston certainly whetted his political appetite, as did the prospect of 'ruffling a few feathers' in the House of Commons. 'I knew I could oust Churchill,' said Clough in his first autobiography. He was even billed as a future minister for sport, but he wasn't convinced that was a serious offer. 'I decided to stick to what I did best – picking football teams.' In October 1974, Churchill's majority was cut to a little over 1,200 by Labour. But by 1979 the previous majority was more than restored as Churchill retained the seat.

Just before Margaret Thatcher came to power in 1979, Clough was apparently seen as a possible key player in the Labour Party's plans to defeat her. It was reported in 2010 that files released by the National Archive disclosed that Labour considered Cloughie a potential ally in the 1979 general election.

'Brian Clough and Marjorie Proops are possibles (Elton John is said to be Labour, but has a complicated image),' said the briefing document, released under the government's 30-year rule at the time.

Strangely enough, Margaret Thatcher was in Cloughie's thoughts as part of his regular column for the *Nottingham Evening Post* in October 1991. Brian admitted that if he ever contemplated retirement he would remember Mrs Thatcher. He said, 'I'm going to remember what life has been like for her since she was turfed out of Number 10 by her loyal Party. Absolute purgatory, I'd imagine.' Even as a staunch socialist, Clough said he *almost* felt like shedding a tear for the former PM as he thought about what it would be like for her without 'the trappings of office' along with the sudden loss of status and influence.

'I ask myself what must go through her mind whenever she sees someone sitting in her chair, driving in her car and spending the weekend at Chequers in her place. And I wonder how I'll feel, how I'll react, when my day comes to go.'

His thoughts then quickly switched to his approaching 26th anniversary in management, having started at Hartlepools in October 1965. There was no way he would consider putting his feet up just yet, he said. 'I'm in fine fettle,' he added, jokingly stating that he was in such a positive frame of mind that he might even attend *all* board meetings, despite his loathing of them.

Clough's hopes for the future went even further. His ambition was to surpass Billy Walker as Nottingham Forest's longest-serving manager. Indeed, he was counting down the days: four years, two months and 12 days, to be precise. But the aim of beating Walker's 21 years was to elude him. Retirement came in May 1993 after a remarkable 18 years. His trophy collection easily outstripped his predecessors and the transformed City Ground stadium stands as an impressive legacy.

* * *

I don't doubt for a second that Brian Clough would have made a great politician. He would easily have torn a strip off some of those who've been in power. Back in 1970, Clough admitted that he would have had no hesitation in becoming prime minister – if a job swap had been available! Admittedly, the comment was probably 'tongue in cheek' but he agreed with remarks from the prime minister at the time, Harold Wilson, that the job of being a football manager was far riskier than being PM.

Wilson, who had been prime minister since 1964, told *Goal* magazine, 'If I were a football manager, on present form I would be more worried about job security than I am as prime minister.'

In response, Clough told the *Daily Mirror*, 'In politics you have to get elected to start with, of course. But once in, you are there for five years at least. In football you might sign a five-year contract but whether you last out is another thing.

'The only job I can think of that is less secure than football manager is snow-clearing.' But Brian added, 'Of course, I wouldn't mind swapping jobs with the prime minister.'

However, he may have changed his mind shortly after that interview. Just two months later, Wilson lost the general election to Edward Heath. Nevertheless, the insecurity facing football managers was an issue that often led to Clough making the headlines.

In September 1980, ahead of a home match against Manchester City, he was typically forthright in his views, speaking about what he described as the 'directors' noose'. In his programme notes, Clough expressed concern that the 'fatality rate among football managers is reaching the levels of about one a day'.

He listed the names of various bosses who had recently received the chop, including Bill McGarry at Newcastle, Jimmy Adamson at Leeds and Bristol City's Alan Dicks.

'We are all asking who is next because in all honesty nobody knows where the scaffolding is being erected,' said Clough, before adding it was a fate that all managers would face 'somewhere along the line' even if they'd already been sacked at a previous club.

Clough also asked readers to stop and think about the effects on the lives of managers who were 'kicked out of a job'.

'I know how I felt when Leeds showed me the door – and don't say I was laughing all the way to the bank. Financial settlements might soften the blow in certain areas but it's far from everything in my book.' He admitted it was a hazard they all accepted.

Clough then kicked the ball firmly back into the boardroom, saying managers 'can't help wondering when the next chairman will find HIS neck in a noose!'

While researching this book, I came across another golden quote, as Cloughie spoke to Sky Sports in 2003 about the managerial merry-go-round at Derby County, 'Derby County are going through managers like my two-month-old granddaughter goes through nappies.'

In January the previous year, Brian criticised the board of directors at Derby for parting company with Colin Todd. 'Sacking someone after just 90 days in charge is ludicrous,' Clough told the *Daily Mirror*. 'The directors have got it all hopelessly wrong. The most important thing they ever have to do is appoint the manager. Colin Todd is the second one they have got rid of this season.' Clough added that Todd's successor would face a tough task. 'It will be difficult enough for the poor bloke to win a single match, never mind keep Derby in the Premiership. He will have an impossible job, an horrendous task.' Todd's replacement, John Gregory, lasted just 14 months in the job.

* * *

Among the many political subjects Clough commented on over the years, perhaps the following observations about the National Health Service are the most poignant. It's nearly 50 years since these words were spoken but they are still relevant today. I would have loved to hear his opinions on how modern-day doctors and nurses have been forced to go on strike in order to highlight the issue of pay.

Referring to the Labour politician Aneurin Bevan, who established the NHS in the first place, Clough said in 1975, 'This is the biggest gift he could have given us, outside of breathing oxygen – and that's also free.'

Clough went on to describe Bevin as a staggering man and said it was a major achievement that the NHS had continued to survive, despite all its problems. 'And long may it continue to survive,' he said.

Then came a remark which should never be forgotten when assessing the importance of the NHS, 'If we lose that type of thing in this country then perhaps we'll have lost a million years of progress.'

The struggles of working people were never lost on Cloughie. Having come from a working-class family, with five brothers and two sisters, he had experienced life at the sharp end. His was a happy childhood, with the family's summer holiday to Blackpool being a highlight of the year. Christmas usually meant a stocking containing a tangerine, some nuts, an apple and a packet of sweets (his dad Joe worked at the local sweet factory). Right at the bottom of the stocking would be a two-shilling piece or an old half-crown. His dad would go to the bank to ensure the coins were shiny new ones.

Brian's friend Colin Shields told me how they would talk about politics during car journeys around the country – and sometimes on the way to radio phone-ins, to get him 'warmed up' for his discussions with listeners. Colin joined him on the election trail, canvassing on behalf of Labour candidates. Brian also helped the Derby MP Philip Whitehead retain his seat, having never forgotten the support that the parliamentarian had given him following his resignation from Derby County. Mr Whitehead was said to have described Brian's impact in glowing terms, saying he had drawn people out to vote like the Pied Piper.

Cloughie joined marches in support of striking miners and handed out free match tickets to their families and those affected by the collapse of Rolls Royce in Derby in the early 1970s. In September 1984 Clough was pictured welcoming the families of striking miners to the City Ground. It wasn't the first time that he had hosted the children of mining families during the dispute, and in return he was presented with a set of miniature miners' lamps. 'We have close associations with the mining community because a lot of our supporters are involved in the industry,' he said. 'It gave me a lot of pleasure to entertain the kids and I hope their visit to the ground gave them a bit of a lift.'

But when the choice came between politics and football, it was football success that would always be his ultimate goal. 'Politics has been an interest, yes,' he reflected, 'but I could never allow it to occupy too much time in my life.'

23

An Angel For Cloughie

'Roy Keane' was the shout from a member of the audience, when Clough was asked who had been the most difficult player to manage during his career. But Brian wasn't having any of it. He told the football forum, 'Roy was an angel with me.' Despite an incident in Jersey when he sent Keane home, Clough said he couldn't fault the young Irishman's desire, talent and professionalism. 'He was good – and he was good with me,' added Brian.

'I signed him when he was 17 years old and he was a bit wary of me, to be fair. I got his mam and dad over from Ireland to try to help him feel at home. I was going through a stage when I was managing very young players. I told him to get himself a girl in Nottingham. If you settle down at home with your family, it's conducive to good football. If you come home and there's a smiling face from your wife and children, it's utopia. He's settled down now.' And to just make the audience laugh, Clough added, 'I think he's reached the stage where he thinks he can play.'

At the time of the forum in 2002, Keane was at Manchester United but was facing a spell on the sidelines for too many bookings. 'I think over the last year or so, Alex [Ferguson] should have put his arm around him and said, "Hey, come on, just calm down a wee bit." Keane's all right, he just needs an arm around the shoulder. He needs a little bit of guidance. He's in a big, dirty city called Manchester and he just needs help.'

Keane has always spoken warmly of the way Clough guided him during his early days at Nottingham Forest and launched his career in English football. Speaking in 2010, before a visit to the City Ground as Ipswich manager, Keane told a news conference, 'I went back before with Sunderland and I could feel the man in the building, especially when I walked into the dressing room area.'

Keane said he loved his three years working with Clough, 'A brilliant, brilliant manager. The man was a genius. He was good to me, good to my family, he never lied to me, he treated me with respect and gave me time off when I was homesick. He didn't give me too much money early on, he was clever like that, a clever, clever man. He knew his football and on top of that he had good coaching staff.' Arriving as a teenager from Ireland, Keane said he appreciated how Clough hadn't overcomplicated the game, 'What I remember most about him was how he kept it simple. But maybe that was just with me because he felt that was all I could understand! Before my debut at Liverpool he said, "All I want you to do is pass to a red shirt." We were playing in red that day. I said, "I think I can do that," and I did it for the next 17 or 18 years, passing and moving.'

The way Cloughie introduced Keane to first-team football was inspired. I've read stories in which the established players at the time didn't really know who he was when he travelled up with them on the team coach for that Liverpool match. But Brian's friend Colin Shields told me how he helped the young midfielder get to Anfield separately by car, unaware that he was about to make his debut.

Colin recalled it was August 1990, 'It was a masterstroke of man-management by Brian because Roy didn't realise he was playing until the last minute. It meant there was no time for him to get nervous. In fact, I travelled up to Liverpool with Roy that day and neither of us had the faintest idea he would be making an appearance on the Anfield pitch. We thought he was going along just for the experience of it.' On the day of the match, Colin had arrived at Brian's house in Derby, when his assistant Ron Fenton also turned up along with two players, including Roy.

'Brian gave him a glass of milk to drink – I think Roy was a bit reluctant at first but he drank it,' said Colin. 'We then made our way up to Liverpool and I was in the same car as Ron and Roy. Ron was chatting away with me during the journey but I think Roy was fairly quiet and didn't say a lot. As it turned out, he did all his talking on the pitch that night. He had only found out about an hour before kick-off that he was going to play.'

Cloughie's former chief scout, Maurice Edwards, continued the story, explaining that Keane thought he was simply helping behind the scenes at Anfield, 'When Clough asked, he explained he was assisting Liam O'Kane laying out the kit in the dressing room. Clough told him, "That's great! But you see that number six shirt son, you will be wearing that tonight."'

Edwards added, 'Roy sat down, went ghostly white and said, "What, me?" Brian said, 'Yes, you son.'" When the other players returned from the warm-up, Clough told them that 'the Irishman' would be making his debut and Phil Starbuck would also be playing – and the team were to look after them.

'As the bell rang in the dressing room for the players to make their way out on to the pitch, Brian said, in his inimitable way, "Irishman come here," then proceeded to give him a big hug and a kiss, and said "Go and enjoy it, son." The match ended in a 2-0 defeat but it was the start of a wonderful career.'

Keane's arrival at Forest had been thanks to a scout who had spotted him playing for Cobh Ramblers in a youth cup match in Ireland. The *Sunday Independent* in Dublin reported how, although the Ramblers had lost 4-0, the scout – Noel McCabe – was so impressed by Keane's performance that he arranged for him to spend the following week with the Reds. The newspaper cutting, from January 1991, described how Roy was about to embark on his first English FA Cup match, against Crystal Palace. It read, 'Keane, who was a Spurs fan until he signed for Forest, is on the crest of a wave at present, having scored four goals in his last four games. Significantly, he has been moved into a central midfield role, having begun his first-team career playing in either of the wide positions.'

The article described him as 'a modest lad' who said he had done 'nothing special – not yet'. Indeed, I remember meeting him briefly around that time outside the Robin Hood Club at the City Ground. He came across as quite a shy but very polite young man. The newspaper report added that Keane was planning a few days back visiting Cork and would visit his friends at Cobh Ramblers, quoting him as saying, 'Because they were great for me.'

Maurice Edwards told a wonderful story of how Brian was so keen (excuse the pun) to watch his new signing play that he interrupted a friendly match in order to bring him on. Clough had given instructions for reserve team coach Archie Gemmill to put Keane into the side at half-time, but when the second half began the new recruit was not on the pitch.

'Brian jumped out of his seat and shouted, "There's no Irishman!" He jumped over the low fence on to the pitch and asked the referee, Brian Saunders, to stop the game. Brian yelled to the bench, "Young Gemmill off, Irishman get on!"' Cloughie was referring to Archie's son, Scott Gemmill.

'Roy showed his qualities and Brian was very impressed with what he saw,' said Edwards. 'After the game, Brian reminded Archie with a few choice words that when he gave orders, they were to be carried out.'

As with the senior players, Clough was determined to keep young Keane's feet firmly on the floor. In fact, so firm that they wouldn't be doing cartwheels or anything similar. Despite scoring the winning goal in 1-0 FA Cup quarter-final against Norwich in 1991, Roy received a telling off for overdoing his celebration, his manager saying, 'If he wants to do somersaults, I'll get him fixed up with a job in a circus.' Clough said later, 'No one played the big-time Charlie at my club.'

During a particularly difficult time for Keane at Manchester United, Brian suggested Sir Alex Ferguson should give him a wallop. 'I only ever hit Roy the once. He got up so I couldn't have hit him very hard,' recalled Clough. Speaking in September 2002, he told the *Sunday People*, 'I think Alex should threaten Keaney and say, "If you don't put your house in order you're going back to Cloughie for a month." That'll make him bloomin' think.' Many years later, Keane defended his old boss and said the punch was probably deserved. 'The odd punch didn't do any harm,' he told Sky Sports in 2023. 'I gave a short back-pass against Crystal Palace which led to an equaliser – which wasn't my fault – and after the match he punched me.'

When Keane was sent home from the 2002 World Cup, Old Big 'Ead supported the decision by Ireland boss Mick McCarthy to send his captain packing after a row. Brian said that if he'd been in McCarthy's position Keane would have to apologise 'on his hands and knees at my feet' to be allowed back in the squad. But there was no hiding Clough's admiration for his former player, when he told the *Sunday Express* in the same article, 'I have always rated Roy as arguably the best midfielder in the Premiership, if not the world. The lad is that good.'

In one of the archive recordings in my collection, dated September 2003, Clough was asked whether he'd spoken to Keane recently. Brian said they'd not had a conversation since he left Forest, 'To be fair, I didn't talk to him much when he worked for me. He was a young, shy lad and he didn't talk very much at all. But he did what's most important for footballers, he did his talking on the field.' Clough said Keane had been a superb player, even at 18 years old, 'When I see him, he'll probably give me a slight grin like he used to when he was player … deep down I think he's a smashing fella.'

The admiration was mutual. Keane told a news conference, 'You look at what Brian Clough achieved and it's scary. Winning the European Cup back to back with a club like Forest, unbelievable. I don't think we'll ever appreciate what the man did.'

I can't help thinking how entertaining it would have been to hear them both talking together about football these days. I would gladly have paid a subscription to watch that programme. So it was fitting that Roy picked Brian as one of his four guests for a 'dream dinner party'. Alongside Diego Maradona and the singers Bob Dylan and Bruce Springsteen, the Sky Sports pundit said on Sky show *The Overlap* that he would invite Cloughie too, 'Just because I'm a bit older now so I can have a good conversation with him. When you're a kid and they're your manager, your boss, you're frightened to death of them. Just to have a normal, proper, decent conversation with him.'

I've no doubt Cloughie would have loved it too.

With thanks to: the Clough family for their continued support, Matt Wilkinson from Rogues Gallery, Steve Caron at JMD Media, my editors Gareth Davis & Michelle Grainger plus designer Matthew Limbert; Natalie Fahy from the *Nottingham Post*, Mark Shardlow, Keith Daniell, Chris Ellis, John Lawson, Norman Giller, Mike West, Colin Shields, Roland Clarke, Carl Savill, Billy Lundy, Sam Moore and everyone else who's helped along the way.

Bibliography

Broadcasters and shows:
BBC Radio Nottingham
BBC Radio Derby
BBC Radio 4
BBC Radio 5 Live
106 Century FM (East Midlands)
Sky Sports
BBC *Football Focus*
talkSPORT
RamsTV

Newspapers/magazines/websites:
brianclough.com
Daily Mirror
Nottingham Post
Football Post
Evening Standard
Liverpool Echo
The Guardian
The Sun
Daily Express
BBC *Match of the Day* magazine (year 2000)
FourFourTwo magazine
Nottingham Forest matchday programmes (various 1975–2004)
Shoot! magazine

ONZE magazine (France)
Goal! magazine
national-football-teams.com
dcfc.co.uk
insidethegames.biz

Books:
Clough – The Autobiography, Brian Clough (Corgi Books)
On Days Like These, Martin O'Neill (Pan Macmillan)
Brian Clough: Fifty Defining Fixtures, Marcus Alton (Amberley Publishing)
Rats, Pies and Pigeon Poo, Dennis Coath (Olympia Publishers)
Jimmy Greaves: The One And Only, Norman Giller (Pitch Publishing)
My Magic Carpet Ride, Garry Birtles (Reid Publishing)
Super Tramp, John Robertson (Mainstream Publishing)
Nobody Ever Says Thank You, Jonathan Wilson (Orion Books)
Forever Forest, Don Wright (Amberley Publishing)
The Day I Met Brian Clough, Marcus Alton (DB Publishing)
Alchemy, Christopher Hull (The History Press)
Champagne Memories, Colin Shields with Marcus Alton (DB Publishing)
A Right Pair, Maurice Edwards (DB Publishing)
Derby County: The Complete Record (Breedon Books)

Podcasts/videos/DVDs/CDs:
Green Jumper podcast
Cloughie – The Brian Clough Story (Watershed Pictures)
Champions of Europe, 25 Years On (The Media Group)

#StandTogether – Grant's Whisky UK and Archie Gemmill (YouTube, 2014)
The Overlap (available on YouTube)

Clough – The Greatest England Manager That England Never Had (ITV Sport, 2009)
Local Heroes (Krafty Entertainment Ltd, 2023)
nicktimo11 (YouTube)
Brian Clough, In His Own Words (BBC/AudioGo)

Printed in Great Britain
by Amazon

39722924R00110